Being Afraid but Freaking Doing It Anyway:

Freedom From Your Narcissist!

Georgina Twumasi

ISBN: **978-1-955312-67-7**

Printed in the United States of America

Story Corner Publishing & Consulting, Inc.

Chesapeake, VA 23321

Storycornerpublishing@yahoo.com

www.StoryCornerPublishing.com

Dedication

This book is dedicated to my momma. She inspired me to be great no matter what the circumstances. She fought and sacrificed so much for me and my siblings. Although my mom lost herself and her glow along the way, I will hold on to my memories of her and light the torch for the generations of women to follow. May God's grace continue to be with my mom and smile down on me and all women in the world.

Love you, Mom!

Table of Contents

Introduction

As a psychiatric provider, you hear so many stories. Some seem like a fairytale because they sound so unbelievable. In a fairytale, there are highs and lows. Most fairytales end in "happily ever after," but the ones I hear are never as such. Sometimes I wish I had never heard their stories because they stuck with me for some time. I guess that is why others need to talk about their problems so they can be released from their minds.

I remember this woman named Liza who walked into my office over 20 times. She would discuss how broken and victimized she had been since her husband left her. Liza expressed that her ex-husband and her mother, (the flying monkey or spy) were narcissistic friends working against her. A flying monkey is a term used in the context of narcissistic abuse to describe individuals who support and enable the abuser. They act as allies or enablers of the narcissist, often carrying out their manipulative tactics and furthering their agenda.

Liza's ex-husband even succeeded in turning their children against her and none of them bothered to call her for over 10 years. She did not even get calls on her birthday. Liza did not have much money so she could not afford a lawyer who would truly fight on her behalf. Liza felt lost and stuck in the shadows of her ex-husband because he took everything. Although he had moved on and seemed to enjoy his new life with another woman, Liza still felt she had to submit to his every word to keep the peace. She would sometimes cry the entire session because she could not put into words how she felt. Liza would sit and stare dissociated out the window as if she was not even in the office. She even expressed how she was trying to stop drinking. Liza started drinking to escape the reality of her life as she knew it. This was an example of many stories I would hear from women all the time! The women would be so broken and stuck in a victim mindset. They end up believing this narrative would follow them for the rest of their lives and they would never gain enough strength to awaken from the nightmare.

I would always think to myself as I heard their stories, "How could one get so broken without seeing the red flags from the beginning?" This got me thinking. How do we women find ourselves so stuck in the dark that we forget light ever existed? Why do we allow the ones who are supposed to protect and love us to beat us down so badly? I had so many questions and just could not wrap my mind around it. I wanted to give the best advice possible, but I just couldn't understand what shifted in their relationship. Most of the relationships failed between 5 and 15 years, but why not sooner? Liza's story really touched me in a way that I can't explain. I took as many notes as I could per session and started my journey of research until I realized Liza and I had so much in common.

Just when I thought my life couldn't get any better, my life came crumbling down like Liza's in the blink of an eye. I could not believe I fell prey to the narcissist! I thought I paid enough attention to details which would've made me less vulnerable, but truthfully, I now know anyone could fall victim. My marriage started perfectly then the gates of hell released every demon to try to kill me. I had to fight for my freedom and my innocent children. It wasn't an easy road. My fight started when I couldn't take it anymore. I did not want to lose myself as Liza did by being broken into tiny unrecognizable pieces. I had to hold onto what little bit of me I had left to get out as best I could.

Ladies, it's time to search within and take a stand! Enough is enough and you deserve the best. Take hold of your life and happiness. It is possible to leave the past and walk into the future with zeal and certainty. This story is about a woman who beat the odds that were stacked against her. She went through hell and back, but God was with her every step of the way and rescued her at her lowest moments. She was afraid that she would fail and become another casualty of a narcissist, but with God, faith, dedication, and resilience all things are possible.

Doing it afraid means to move in faith. No matter how long you wait for the "right moment" you may never truly feel ready. Fear is only "False Evidence Appearing Real." I know you may be afraid of the circumstances you are facing but do it anyway! It will pay off in the long run and you will be an example to many who are suffering.

Chapter 1

Seeds of Trauma and Pain

There was a girl who dreamed she could and so she did. This girl was depressed and had a poor sense of self. She had to figure out how to turn it all around. Too many things were going wrong in her life and at one point she thought that was all life had to offer. This girl was who I used to be. I went from having nothing to being the boss of my own company today. This is my testimony of what faith and resilience looks like after many trials.

I remember my childhood as a time of bitterness, depression, and extreme sadness, interrupted only by fleeting moments of joy. We lived in poverty, surviving on hand-me-downs that others could no longer wear. As a family of eight, we relied on local food pantries and churches for basic necessities. My father's friends would sometimes offer us their old clothes if they had any to spare. I was grateful to be alive, but I couldn't accept that this was all life had to offer. Even as a child, I knew there had to be more.

Despite my longing for change, everything was out of my control. My parents, though well-intentioned, seemed trapped, lacking the knowledge, motivation, or resources to lift us out of poverty. I often wondered what I could do to make our situation better. Looking back now, I suppose they did the best they could with what they had, but at the time, it felt like a cruel, unbreakable cycle. Many nights, I believed my life was cursed, and thoughts of death crept into my mind. Hunger was a constant companion. When my father couldn't borrow money from friends, we went to bed with empty stomachs or scavenged whatever we could from my mother's small garden. Those nights taught me a harsh but valuable lesson, nothing is handed to you in life; you must work for it.

From as far back as I can remember, my parents struggled to make ends meet. We lived in a cramped one-bedroom house, barely managing to keep a roof over our heads. Every month, the landlord threatened eviction, but perhaps out of pity, he would grant my father an extra week to come up with the rent. I often feared we would end up homeless, but somehow, we always held on—if only by a thread. My father worked long hours, but his wages were never enough. My mother, in her own way, tried to contribute. She sold platters of stinky fish, tomatoes, and hot peppers in front of our house, desperately attempting to bring in extra income. Looking back, I suppose one could call her an entrepreneur. Yet, no matter how hard they worked, it was never enough to escape the crushing weight of poverty.

Money—or the lack of it—was the root of constant arguments between my parents. My siblings and I dreaded those nights when their voices would rise in anger, the air in our tiny home thick with tension. My father, burdened by stress and frustration, was often on edge. His anger became a force we learned to avoid, a storm we could not stop. I remember trembling at the sound of his raised voice, knowing that any wrong move could set him off. The trauma of my childhood left a lasting imprint on me—mentally, emotionally, and even physically. Despite the chaos, my siblings and I searched for moments of happiness wherever we could find them. When my father wasn't home, my sister and I held dance competitions in the living room, our small radio becoming our most prized possession. We clung to these brief escapes, pretending, if only for a moment, that we were just like other children—carefree and full of laughter.

Yet, beneath the surface, we were all drowning in pain. I cried myself to sleep more nights than I could count. My mother, overwhelmed by trauma and depression, slowly retreated into herself. There were days when she wouldn't speak at all, disappearing into a silent world of her own. My father, on the other hand, battled his demons outwardly—his pride, his disappointments, his crushed self-esteem. I believe he felt like less of a man because he couldn't provide for us the way he wanted to. The weight of his failures consumed him, and instead of seeking help or change, he let his bitterness take root. He had opportunities to go back to school, to travel abroad, to build a better life for us— but fear and complacency held him back. He convinced himself that poverty was his fate. "Que Será, Será—whatever will be, will be," he would say. I despised that mindset. I knew that life didn't have to be this way, and I vowed that when I grew up, I would never live like this.

The deeper we sank into poverty, the darker my father became. The stress overtook his mind, transforming him into a stranger— someone we feared rather than relied on. He should have been our protector, but instead, he became a force we had to protect ourselves from. In our culture, women and children had no voice, and my father had zero tolerance for opinions, let alone "backtalk." He saw any questioning of our circumstances as an attack on his pride. The more we struggled, the more he withdrew into despair.

In my country, no matter how a parent raises their child, that child is expected to care for them in old age. Sometimes I had my reservations, but I know God is watching. Therefore, I will continue to make sure my parents are good. As a child, I couldn't comprehend the weight my parents carried, the stress, the sacrifices, the quiet frustration. But now, as an adult with a family of my own, I see it more clearly. Life is about making the right choices and one bad choice could have you dealing with years of recovery. Although years later, my father apologized for acting out in rage, the scars remain. Forgiveness came, yet the memories lingered, shaping us in ways we never anticipated. I longed to be free—free from the pain, the fear, the trauma that clung to me like a shadow. For years, I couldn't even bring myself to speak about my past. It was easier to bury it deep within me and surrender it to God.

Childhood trauma is often ignored, dismissed as something children simply "grow out of." But I am living proof that what happens in your early years can shape your entire future. It affects your mental health, your relationships, and your self-worth. If more people acknowledged the lasting impact of childhood trauma, perhaps we could break the cycle—preventing future generations from carrying the same burdens of pain and silence.

Yet, in my country, there are deeper wounds that no one dares to address. Rape, molestation, sexual perversion, and even sex trafficking are grim realities, but they remain taboo. Fear, shame, and cultural conditioning silence the victims before they even find their voices. Women, especially, are taught submission from a young age—indoctrinated into believing they must endure whatever happens to them without resistance. One in three homes experience multiple forms of abuse, yet the community remains silent. Everyone knows, but no one intervenes. And the ones who suffer the most? The children.

What could we do? If we spoke out, who would listen? Who would help? The legal system was corrupt, offering no refuge. The police were just as dangerous as the criminals. We had no one. We were forced to accept our reality, to survive in a world where justice was a privilege reserved for the powerful. But I refused to let my past define me. I fought to break free. And though the scars remain, I stand as living proof that survival is possible—that healing is possible. I am not merely a product of my trauma; I am a testament to resilience, strength, and the unyielding determination to create a better future.

What is childhood trauma?

"The experience of an event by a child that is emotionally painful or distressful, which often results in lasting mental and physical effects." – The National Institute of Mental Health: definition of childhood trauma.

Childhood trauma occurs due to the impression or shock of the event, which causes the child to develop psychological and even interpersonal trauma. Interpersonal trauma is that which originates in the child's relationships. Examples of interpersonal trauma include emotional, physical, or sexual abuse; experiencing or witnessing violence within the family, home, or community (e.g., civil disturbances, armed conflict, death.) A child who is emotionally or physically neglected may also develop trauma. Trauma is an injury to your nervous system and affects your hormones, psychological state, and immune system. Trauma even brings on some degree of learning disability, ADHD (attention deficit disorder), increased risk of early dementia, lupus, multiple sclerosis, fertility issues, foggy brain, and CPTSD. Trauma ruins lives, relationships, and careers. It can even cause addiction, and it is the number one diagnosis of people incarcerated. CPTSD is chronic stress as a result of being exposed to trauma over a long period.

Look over your life. Think about some of the unfavorable situations you have encountered. Did you ever put them in the trauma category? Or maybe you thought it was just life and everyone goes through the things you went through. Some things can be prevented with proper healing and other things are brought on by those who do not know any better and continue to pass down generational curses. Did you grow up faced with abuse, neglect, poverty, or exposure to violence, addiction, or alcoholism? Did you grow up with parents who were incarcerated, or parents with severe mental health issues that were left untreated? Did your parents go through a tumultuous divorce that left years of scars? Have you suffered from other chronic or intense stress? All these situations open the door to trauma. Trauma is more detrimental to our health than we think.

Do you sometimes get overwhelmed by your emotions, in a way that you might describe as "over-sensitive" or "over-reactive?" When you get into a dark mood, do you have trouble getting out of it? Do you have problems with memory, paying attention, or working consistently on tasks until they're complete? Do you suffer from anxiety, depression, addiction, drug, or alcohol problems of your own? Does the way you express anger cause problems in your relationships, your work, or your life? Does your mind sometimes feel like a "hamster wheel" of anxious thoughts, making it hard to relax or sleep when it's time? Do you instinctively crave an easy or natural way to calm your brain and emotions so you can start feeling happier and free from old problems? Well, you have experienced trauma in your life, and it has affected you in some form or fashion. The good news is there is help for you.

I did not know much about my trauma responses, codependency, trauma bonding, or anxious attachment issues I had adopted back then when I was ignorant of trauma existing. I thought it was just life and I had to take it and move on, but I did not know that I could release the trauma to become free. After experiencing trauma in my childhood, my adult life was upside down for over fifteen years. I'm sure the process doesn't take that long for the average person to be healed, but I went through so much and did not have anyone to coach me through. I did not have a lot of information concerning trauma nor did I know it was an issue that was affecting me. I noticed negative patterns within my behavior. I would get overwhelmed with my emotions when the trauma was triggered. Every time I thought I moved on from the hurt, something would be done or said to me that made me think of all that had happened to me in the past. Placing everything in a pot only overflowed in my mind at the wrong times or times when I had enough! It would be hard to come out of the dark place I chose to go to once something frustrated me or fear entered my mind. My mind was all over the place and I could not focus on a task or complete one on time. I suffered from anxiety, depression, and addiction. Anger took over me and I could not control it once I was backed into a corner or pushed over the edge.

I could barely sleep and was restlessly fighting thoughts in my mind. Many things became triggers for me until I started healing from the trauma. It was not until I was fully healed that I could breathe and press forward again in life. I had to let go of those things that caused me pain and allow God to heal me from the inside out. I took many steps around God because society had a set blueprint to follow for healing, but I found myself exhausting a lot of money, time, and resources to still end up seeking God. Once I surrendered all I knew, all I thought, and what people said to God, I prayed and asked God to help me and He did. Allow me to share my journey with you just so you know this isn't another one of those "get healed quick schemes" so I can take all your money. No, I pray you all are healed because of reading this book and applying the tools that are listed to your journey. I even pray the trauma you faced doesn't push you into the arms of a narcissist or someone who will only take advantage of you. If you have already fallen prey, I hope these tools serve as fuel for you to get out of your current situation!

Healing from childhood trauma

1. **Learn as much as you can about trauma and triggers.** The more informed you are the better you will become at recognizing the red flags. Read "The Body Keeps the Score" by Bessel Van Der Kolk and "Complex PTSD" by Pete Walker. There are many other great books out there, but I started with these books. Also, take the ACE's survey to get a better idea of what level of trauma you experienced so that you can counteract to preserve your health and mental state.

2. **Acknowledge your triggers and learn to control your reactions.** Keep in mind what makes you upset or causes

fear then mark boundaries. Teach people how to properly handle you by accepting what you like and voicing and shutting down what you don't like. When you continue to emotionally spiral out of control, you put your nervous system at risk for damage. Neurological Dysregulation Syndrome (NDS) is the result of tension in the nervous system causing an imbalance of neurological function. Nervous system dysregulation (NSD) is a term used to describe a set of symptoms that develop after a stressful or traumatic event or after experiencing a prolonged period of stress. It means that the nervous system is constantly in a state of either fight-or-flight or shutdown/freeze, which can lead to health problems and inappropriate or disproportionate responses to situations. NSD can be caused by unresolved stress responses from the past or by other factors that affect the nervous system's function. Nervous system regulation is a key component of healing and maintaining good mental health.

3. **Detach from negative people and conversations.** Boundaries are expressed in many ways. Removing or closing the door to people, places, and things that mean you no good is the quickest way to see results on your healing journey. When you see the pattern of red flags, it is time to move on, especially among friends and people you date. While dating, this is the time to observe and get to know

others on a deeper level. Dating is the perfect time to look for red flags or things you do not like so you can decide if you want to go further with that person. Dating reveals the true person over time so do not rush through that process. Do not sacrifice your peace to make others happy. If they love you, they will want you to be at peace as well.

4. **Be ok with being alone and getting to know yourself.** I remember getting into the most drama and enduring unforgettable pain when I was desperate for company. I thought I needed friends, relationships, or someone to talk to to validate who I am. I would attend social events I hated, just to be around a crowd. I hung onto friends and men who did not add to my purpose because I did not feel comfortable alone. Therefore, I found myself willing to please others at my own expense so they wouldn't leave me. I had to train myself day after day to be alone and then do things alone. After a while it became a habit, then anxiety and stress decreased over time. In my alone time, I learned more about myself. I learned what I liked and didn't like. I'm not saying to isolate yourself from others forever, but do not become codependent on others. Life is about balance and there is a time for everything. I can even take trips, go on dates, hang out, etc. alone, and not think twice about it.

5. **Stop spending all your hard-earned money on therapy and food to try to heal.** Understand life has challenges and people who are toxic because it brings balance. Where there is good, there is also bad. I thought I would go through life dodging evil situations if I continued to be good to others, but that was not the case. Bad things happen to everyone. It is how you deal with it that matters. When I felt stressed, I tried anything to make the pain go away including therapy and excessive eating. Everyone recommends going to therapy when someone expresses a problem they cannot handle. I'm sure therapy has helped some people, but it did not always work for me. I sometimes found myself worse off than when I started. Therapy is only a tool to take off the band-aid by going back down memory lane with no effective solutions to start healing. Therefore, after I talked about my problems, they would just sit in my mind tormenting me. The memories would affect my day, mood, and the way I handled other people days later. Therapy alone does not heal the past trauma you may have faced. Sure, it's good to talk about your problems so you could try to make sense of them, but without a blueprint to get to the next step, you could be stuck with the thoughts. I also tried to eat my pain away, but I'm sure you could see how that is not good for our health. My body was impacted negatively due to all the weight I gained and all the unhealthy comfort foods I consumed. There is no such thing as eating your pain away. You only become

overweight and unhealthy. We should eat to live, not eat for comfort or out of routine. I recommend taking a holistic approach to soothing your pain such as cryotherapy, EMDR, CBT therapy, eye movement, and acupuncture. It helps your mind and body to reset after conflict.

6. **Exercise daily and eat healthy.** No one ever told me about the positive effects exercise has on your mind and body. Exercise is great for re-regulating your body, calming emotions, and maintaining healthy lungs, muscles, and a healthy heart. Weightlifting challenges the mitochondria in the muscles which release good endorphins including dopamine and serotonin in our brain. This helps us continually feel good about ourselves. Now that I exercise daily, I have so much more confidence and energy. I feel more gorgeous and healthier, even though I'm much older now. Eating healthy helps my body to run smoothly and even my thoughts. Almost every food today has chemicals in it or on it, so strive to eat the best which minimizes your exposure to too many chemicals. Some chemicals react poorly within your body and cause an imbalance in your mind. Therefore, be mindful of that as well. It's important to take care of your body so it can last and take care of you.

7. **Challenge your perspective on life.** I looked at life through a negative lens because of all the pain that blinded me from

good things. I used to be so pessimistic and judgmental about everything. I had to change the way I thought because everyone is not the same. Just because one person hurt me doesn't mean everyone is out to get me. I had to let my guard down sometimes and give people a chance. I also stopped judging others because life is hard, and no one knows what they would do unless they walk through the situation in question. I'd completely embraced the understanding that most things are complicated, and people work out things the best way they can. Everything is not always black and white. It's best to have compassion for everyone. I'd quit being so judgmental and telling others how they should live because I needed to work on myself. I also had to give myself grace through my healing journey. Not everything happens overnight. I even make sure to only indulge in positive things such as optimistic conversations, music, shows, and movies. I took a stand with deleted all music representing death, heartache, betrayal, crazy love, revenge, and self-pity. No longer will that keep my focus on negativity and I will continue to replace bad habits with good ones. Positive vibes only.

8. **Be the change you want to see.** Be what you seek. Do what you want from others. Do unto others how you want to be treated. Don't wait for others to give to you before you extend yourself. Even Jesus Christ came into the world not to

be served, but to serve others. God knows what you need, and you will get it in due time, but you cannot get things with a selfish heart. Life is not just about you and your needs or desires. I'm not saying to be a doormat either. Have balance and set healthy boundaries in giving. I wanted nothing more but for true love to find me. Therefore, I started loving myself first and then loving others no matter how I felt. I do not allow a bad day to stop me from loving others. For so long I did not know what true love was until I read this scripture:

"Love is patient, love is kind. It does not envy, it does not boast, it is not proud. It does not dishonor others, it is not self-seeking, it is not easily angered, and it keeps no record of wrongs. Love does not delight in evil but rejoices with the truth. It always protects, always trusts, always hopes, always perseveres. Love never fails..."
1 CORINTHIANS 13:4-8 NIV

9. **Reclaim your control.** When you understand the true meaning of acceptance and letting go, control will be back in your hands. Acceptance means the situation happened and you've decided what you're going to do with it. You can decide to let it rule over your life or you can decide to let it go. You have the control to decide what's next in your life.

10. **Let the right people into your life.** Trauma causes so much pain and fear which convinces us to put up walls and shut everyone out. These bad situations sometimes shape our lives, and we live as victims. We tend not to trust anyone even if they are a good person. Some people are sent into our life to help us and others are sent to hinder us, so it is important to spot the difference. People will show you who they are, you just must pay attention. Do not get caught up in what they say, but what they do. Give grace to allow people to make a mistake. You know who does things on purpose because they continue to cause you pain without remorse. Also, you cannot change anyone, so do not try. People will only change if they truly want it for themselves. Once we change our perspective and the narrative of our lives, we can live as a survivor and overcomer. If you woke up today free from the situation, you are safe. Live your life accordingly.

11. **Get more sleep**. There's not much that a good night or two of decent sleep won't cure. When we get stressed or worried, sleep is the first thing that no longer becomes a priority. Fight the feeling to stay up and do something such as stretches, playing soft instrumental music, praying, or taking a warm bubble bath to wind down from a long day. Do not try to sleep with the television on, drink, do drugs, party during late nights, etc. because that will only take away from your sleep. Lack of sleep drains your body and mind, putting

you at risk for sickness. Good restful sleep is crucial to recovery. Allocating a good six-to-eight-hour sleep pattern is great for the nervous system's recovery. When we sleep, our body heals and rebuilds itself, and our minds can settle from a day of work.

12. **Finally, spiritual guidance**. Life gets rough, and we must release some things to reset our minds. Sometimes we hold things inside that we cannot trust others with. God can give us peace and joy while in a hurt place. He wants the best for us, but we must allow Him into our lives. He knows what we need and is willing to help us. He loves us beyond anything we could imagine. We can connect with God through prayer, reading and studying scriptures, and fasting. Prayer is an intimate conversation with God. He speaks back to us in many ways. He speaks through others, music, signs, dreams, visions, etc. The Bible brings into reality who God is and why we should trust Him. Therefore, reading the Bible helps us to understand why we should allow God into our lives. Fasting is to abstain from food for a certain period. Instead of eating, you would pray and study the Bible to learn more about God. Fasting while praying is a practice done to get more power to fight through fear and thoughts that would set us back from healing.

Once healed from childhood trauma, we will be able to see clearly and perceive things correctly. Looking through pain only causes us to gravitate to the wrong people, places, and things. We then become what hurts us if we are not healed because that's all we have consumed. Predators are always on the prowl and can sense when someone is vulnerable, which makes them an easy target. Trauma distracts us in many ways if we are not healed. Taking the necessary steps to heal helps us to not become easy prey to narcissistic predators.

Chapter 2

Stepping Out on Faith

Healing is an important step in life. It helps one to move forward to achieve greater. Many of us have struggled with a form of trauma. I knew I wanted better for myself, so I had to

of the past and focus on my future. I dreamed of life without misery and imagined myself living in the U.S.A. Most people in my hometown of Ghana would promote how great it was to live in America. They would say America was a place that gave everyone a chance to reach the desires of their heart. They emphasized that America did not enslave women and look down upon them. Instead, they valued women, and every woman had a chance to do things for herself if she chose.

I often daydreamed about how my life would be in the U.S., a faraway country where I could carve my own life. I could call the shots and make necessary changes without feeling like my life was at the mercy of my father who was very controlling. I felt so helpless at times because of poverty, domestic violence, and many environmental stressors living in Ghana. My dreams would include having a man in the house once I moved to the U.S., but if it did not happen, I would've been ok with that too. I had seen from experience that it would have to be the right man, or my life would continue to be a living hell. I was ok with waiting until the right time. I fully support two-parent households and would not have it any other way. I know it is better for the children when parents work together, although this was not the case for my family. I wanted to look past that and have hope that my new home in America would be full of peace and love. I pictured myself in America away from chaos every day and sometimes multiple times a day just to find joy. Honestly, I wish I could have been anywhere but home in Ghana.

I remember one day our neighbor asked me if I ever thought about traveling for college. I asked her for more details, and she told me she was preparing to go to college in America and wondered if I wanted to travel with her. When I heard the word America, I knew my dreams and prayers had been answered. I grew afraid and had no idea where to start. I was a senior in high school and would be graduating in no time. I asked her to help me with the process and I was grateful that she did not hesitate.

She told me the easiest way was to have someone in the U.S. send me an invitation for school purposes. I sat and racked my brain to see who I could ask and then I remembered my uncle who lived in New Jersey. I didn't know him like that so I was afraid he would deny my request. Little did I know that once I stepped out on faith and asked him, he accepted my request. This was the start of my process. I still had to apply for schools and get in. I applied to many schools and finally got accepted to a university in New York. This was problematic for me because I did not have a car to get back and forward from New Jersey to New York, but I was determined to do whatever I had to do to leave Ghana. Gaining admission to the university felt like my ticket out of a war zone.

I did not know how to break the news to my family, but it had to be done. High school was over for me, and it was time to begin my journey of getting out of poverty. I knew I would miss my family very much so I promised to visit as much as I could. They were not very happy to see me go but they understood I needed to make this move. I knew once I left Ghana, I would not be able to return to my family until years later. My journey would be an uphill battle, so I had to stay focused. As an immigrant in America, I would have to fight for my place to become a citizen. I had no idea what I was getting into, but I was willing to learn. The day arrived for me to leave my family in Ghana, I was so heartbroken that I cried every night. I had to keep telling myself this move was for the betterment of myself and my siblings once I could come back for them. The goal was to get out of poverty so that I could help them achieve their dreams. Therefore, I had to take the leap of faith and follow my heart to travel to America.

Once on the plane with my neighbor, I could not believe I was flying. Everything seemed as if I was in a fairytale. It didn't seem real. As a child I imagined living in New York City with all the hustling and skyscrapers. I was waiting to wake up, but that moment never came. The plane landed after hours of travel, and I was off to my uncle's house in New Jersey. America was very different compared to Ghana. I could feel the freedom the moment I stepped off the plane. I was so intrigued with everything. After only a few days in America, I felt liberated, and I was grateful that my uncle allowed me to stay in his home. Classes were soon to begin, and I could not wait to explore. I will never know what I did to deserve such a wonderful blessing, but I was determined not to fail. On my first day of school, I couldn't believe all the people I had seen from Ghana. That was the extra motivation I needed to see. I thought if they could do it, there was no doubt that I could make it. I just had to continue to focus and pace myself accordingly. Most people I met from Ghana stayed on campus, but a few had to commute as I did. Unfortunately, I did not get approved for housing on the campus which would have made life a little easier. All the commuting I had to do cost money, so I needed a job. Over the next two years, I worked and attended school full-time while traveling on multiple buses from sunup to sundown. I never made it home before 10 pm. I was so exhausted but was determined to do whatever I had to do to stay in the U.S.

In my first year, I worked jobs in the mental health field and picked up clients who needed a live-in *Home Health Aid* that was close to my college. After a few years of that, I transitioned to clients who did not need me to live with them so I could start taking classes toward a degree in nursing at the local community college. I worked so hard most days I do not even remember getting any sleep. I did accomplish making it on the Dean's list and I was very proud of myself. I then found an open CNA (Certified Nurse's Assistant) position in the ICU of a hospital which I applied for and got in. I was excited because I knew it was experience towards my nursing degree. I met the supervisor who took me under their wing and trained me for 6months to make sure I was able to work in the ICU as a registered nurse after graduating with my degree.

I pursued my nursing degree over the following five years. It was tough on me because I had to pay out of pocket for the classes. The nursing classes did not meet financial aid's criteria for me to go for free. Nursing school was anything but cheap which meant I had to work longer hours just to take classes. It was my dream, and I did not want it to be wasted. I was determined to chase after it because my family depended on me. Plus, I did not want to move back to Ghana. I did not care what I had to do; I was not going back to Ghana to stay!

I managed to stay on the dean's list and was even chosen to give a speech during my undergraduate graduation.

I eventually acquired my master's degree in nursing, specializing in psychiatry. I then opened my practice, "Psych on Demand" to help people with a variety of mental health challenges. I faced many challenges in between, but I did not allow any of that to stop me. I went from being a CNA to becoming a psychiatric APRN in private practice with my own business. I was even spotlighted and featured on "Great Day Connecticut." I believe in faith, family, and the building of emotional wealth. Good mental health is one of the keys to unraveling many of our suffering in life. As a nurse practitioner, I specialize in psychotropic medications and therapeutic modalities to help individuals achieve their goals in the journey to feeling better. My holistic approach focuses on the mind, body, and soul. Some of the services I offer are:

Medication Management

For many mental health conditions, talk therapy alone may not be enough, this is when we recommend the use of psychotropic medications—those that influence a person's mental state, such as antidepressants—as a treatment option and a complement to talk therapy.

Family Therapy

Family therapy is available to help family members improve communication, resolve conflicts, address co-parenting issues, and find healthy ways to interact.

Couples Therapy

Couples therapy is brief, short-term, and solution-focused so you can start seeing positive results in your relationship right away. These sessions are created to get to the root of the problem so you both can start building a positive future.

Trauma & PTSD Management

Trauma is an emotional response to an event viewed as physically or emotionally threatening or harmful. Trauma can create emotional effects both immediately after the event and in the long term. Trauma can lead to Post-Traumatic Stress Disorder and vicarious trauma. PTSD can develop when symptoms due to the traumatic event continue or increase over time. Vicarious trauma, or secondary trauma, can occur when a person develops trauma symptoms in response to being in close contact with someone who experienced a traumatic event. These sessions are designed to pinpoint the event and start the healing journey.

Depression Treatments

Depression is more than just feeling sad. Depression can lead to a variety of emotional and physical problems that impact your ability to function in your typical day-to-day activities. Depression can be experienced in one episode, but for most, depressive disorder recurs. Approximately 19 million adults and 3 million adolescents experience depressive episodes in the U.S. each year. I've created a holistic approach that treats depression and helps you to live free from the prison in your mind.

Anxiety & Panic Attack Management

Anxiety is a normal response to stress and danger. Anxiety disorder occurs when the level of anxiety interferes with quality of life. Anxiety disorders are the most common mental health disorders affecting approximately 19% of adults and 32% of adolescents in the U.S. each year. We offer healthy management regimens that will allow you to take charge of your life again.

Coaching

Psychological coaching focuses on the positive aspects of the human condition, much like positive counseling; it does not focus on the negative, irrational, and pathological aspects of life. Coaching is specific and goal oriented.

Grief Counseling

Grief is the acute pain that accompanies loss. It reflects what we love, and it can feel all-encompassing. Grief is not limited to the loss of people, but when it follows the loss of a loved one, it may be compounded by feelings of guilt and confusion, especially if the relationship is a difficult one. Many say grief can be overwhelming, but it doesn't have to be. Talking about the situation helps you to put things into the right perspective.

I offer many other services to help others come out of traumatic situations. I value what I do because I know it is needed in the world and helping others is my goal. I did not have many people to help me along my journey in life, but I'm grateful for all those that could help. Most times all I had was God and a prayer. He continued to push me out of fear and into faith. I could not have done any of this without God. Many times, I thought my traumatic experience would keep me enslaved, but God helped along the way. Sure, I lost sight sometimes, but God's grace and love didn't allow me to stay there. We cannot let fear take over our minds. If it's our purpose, the way has already been made for us to succeed. All we must do is keep moving forward in faith. Things will get better.

Fear- an unpleasant emotion caused by the belief that someone or something is dangerous, likely to cause pain or a threat.

False
Evidence
Appearing
Real

Do not allow fear to dictate your life anymore. Take a stand and have faith, then go after what you desire.

Faith- *"Now faith is the substance of things hoped for, the evidence of things not seen."*
Hebrews 11:1 KJV

"And it is impossible to please God without faith. Anyone who wants to come to him must believe that God exists and that he rewards those who sincerely seek him."
Hebrews 11:6 NLT

Chapter 3

Prince Charming

After finally feeling like I was making progress in life, I was open to dating. I remember hanging out with some friends and they wanted to hook me up. They were always talking about this one particular single guy they thought would be a good fit for me. I eventually gave in to see what all the hype was about and boy, I didn't know my life would change forever! When my friends introduced him to me, we hit it off immediately. We both had a lot going on, but we wanted to see each other all the time. We decided to move in together out of convenience although it was never my first thought. I felt I had to make this sacrifice so love would not pass me by. If it didn't work out, we could always just go our separate ways, so I thought.

This man was dreamy, charming, charismatic, optimistic, and a man of faith. He had morals, standards, and goals. That was different for me to experience after the upbringing I experienced, so I was mesmerized and felt I hit the jackpot with a good man. You know, the man every woman dreams of. I was drawn to him and stuck like glue after seeing all the good in him. I didn't want to pass up the opportunity to someone else. I did everything I knew to do to keep this man. I cooked, cleaned, catered to his every need, never told him "No," and made sure our sex life was wild and vibrant. I did not want him to get bored with me, so I was open to exploring his fantasies. I fell in love! I was on cloud 9 for him and if someone I knew saw me, I would've been unrecognizable to them. I could not believe how one simple man had my guard and all my boundaries come tumbling down. I was comfortable with it, but a little nervous at times because it was nothing I ever experienced. All my life I had to live on edge and defense. After being abused, I thought everyone would harm me, so I kept my distance and trusted no one. If I considered you a "friend," I was still reserved and made sure I established boundaries. This man, on the other hand, had my mind and worries gone. I completely let myself go in him. I hung on to every word as if he had a spell on me. He spoke so elegantly, and it was like a melody to my ears. He was everything my father was not, and I loved it. We made lots of plans for our future.

This man was not afraid to take risks and was very confident in himself. He was a natural-born leader that knew what he wanted. He took charge, but not in a pushy way, and always knew what I needed and even made me laugh. He seemed to have everything going for him, so I wondered why he was single. He didn't have any children, women following him, no mother issues, and he was open about himself. We lived together for goodness sake. What could he hide from me? He freely gave so much information to me that I was overwhelmed and thought I should just tell him about my entire self. No need to hide anything because he let so much out. I wanted to be fair and match what he brought to the table so he could realize just how much I was into him. I couldn't believe how honest he was as a man because men get a bad rap when it comes to that. I was thankful I met a different kind of man. I thought it would be years before I found a man to match my energy with striving for goals. I was impressed with every word he spoke. He was very precise in what he said and did. We spent so much time together that I never had to question anything about him. I even found myself bragging about him to others. I could not help myself when I thought of him. He gave me butterflies as if I was a young schoolgirl dancing around the halls. We even started talking about marriage. My heart was so full that I thought I was going to explode every day just looking back over my life. Finally, my dream was complete, and God answered all my prayers. I was in America, completed school, started my dream career, started my own business, and I even have the dream man that I love. All we had to do was get married and start a family.

After months of living on cloud 9 in love, a shift began to occur. I noticed my man becoming stressed and lacking patience when we would just have random conversations. I wanted to help him in any way I could, but it only seemed to make matters worse. I figured I should just back off until he was ready to tell me what was bothering him, but a day turned into a week without words. It seemed strange coming from a man who was very open about everything only to completely shut down. I remember simply asking him what he wanted for dinner, and we got into an intense argument. I had no idea why he got so upset. After asking what was wrong, he just stormed out of the door. I sat up waiting hours for him to come home until I just fell asleep. Sometimes he did not return home for three days at a time. That became his normal pattern for a while. I knew something was not right, but I could not prove anything. I would ask him if he was okay and where he had been, but it would just resort to more intense arguments. I started to feel as if I was the problem and asked him if he wanted to end our relationship, but he would always say he loved me and just needed space.

He was always striving for success and stretching himself in multiple ways to see which area would take off first. He was in school, working towards his career, and desired to open his own business so he could set his own hours. I understood where his mind was because I had been there too. The only difference is I did it alone with no one there to help me. Therefore, I put in as many hours as I could overnight to help him pay for school and get his business off the ground. I wanted to relieve his stress, not make it worse. I loved him, but I wasn't so sure he understood that after a while. It seemed every time he got stressed out, he would take it out on me, but I was only trying to be all he needed. I started thinking I wasn't doing enough. Therefore, I figured if I put in more hours at work so his bills could be paid off quicker, the faster he would get out of the overwhelming cycle of frustration and anxiety. Then we could finally be happy again. So, I worked double shifts and sacrificed my sleep for the one I loved. I wanted the old thing back. I wanted to go back to the way we were before stress and money got in the way. I was willing to do anything for it. I missed how I felt on Cloud 9, but I wondered if it was all just a dream.

I know when people need a break or space, they just want to get away so I tried to be as understanding as I could with him away from the house so often. I didn't want to pry, but I missed him. After working doubles to help him financially all week, I figured I would get to spend time with him on our days off, but that was never the case. He made excuse after excuse. He would say he needed to hang out with his friends or help at church to clear his mind. Soon I felt we were growing apart or maybe I never knew him. We entered the "roommate" stage, but I felt I was carrying the bulk of the weight if it were to be 50/50. After almost a year of this cycle, I couldn't hold my emotions in any longer. I had to come clean because it was eating me alive. After all, we did start the relationship with openness and honesty. I told him if things didn't change, I had to part ways because I did not feel I was with the same man I met back then. He convinced me he would change for the better and he didn't want me to leave, so he asked me to marry him. As much as I wanted to jump for joy, I didn't want to think our marriage would be dysfunctional just as our relationship. I wanted us to be married, healthy, at peace, and happy. I wanted to believe his every word since marriage was a big step. So, I said "yes" because I gave him the benefit of the doubt and had faith in his apology. I was nervous, but I was willing to take a chance. I figured I didn't have anything to lose. I'm sure on the outside looking in someone would call me crazy and think he was manipulating me into marrying him to get my money, but he said he would do the work to change. He expressed how much he loved me, and I wanted to believe him so badly. I could not stop thinking about the beginning of our relationship and the way he made me feel. He swept me off my feet and I felt I was the only one in his world he would go to the ends of the earth to please. What we had was real. Wasn't it? Was I kidding myself? I hoped I was making the right choice. I guess I would never know unless I took the chance, so I did.

We got married and everything was going well for a moment. I thought we could both breathe again and focus on growing together. We continued our financial plan of working as much as we could to get his dreams completed and operating. It was years before we could take a break, but I hung in there and stuck it out with him. We reached "middle-class status" financially and moved into a better area. I was proud of all that we accomplished. We did not have a struggle in sight. Sure, we missed out on a lot of sleep and spending time with each other, but it was worth it if it pleased my husband. Eventually, he obtained his master's degree and opened his business. I was so proud of him and glad we were past the building part of our lives. I was so exhausted, but everything on his goal list was accomplished so he could breathe again. I knew we would go back to living the dream life because nothing major stood in our way. I was so excited to see what our future held, but every conversation was just about his business thriving. I knew what running a business involved because I remembered the long hours I had to put into mine. I know a business is just a full-time job if you are doing everything alone. I was starting to wonder if we would ever spend time together again outside of sleeping in bed together. I say maybe because most times I worked overnight or put in for a double shift that would keep me away from home the entire day. Most times I took a nap at work. Yes, he worked also, but not as many hours as I did. Therefore, I figured he would be the one opting for quality time together because he had more time to rest. I could've easily said I was too tired on my off days and got some sleep, but I didn't want our marriage to fail because of lack of time. I pushed myself to be open for him only to be shot down. He always made me feel that I was asking too much of him, but I didn't want to believe it. I wanted to hang on to the fact that I met a good man with goals and dreams that I wanted him to achieve.

I finally stopped working double shifts and only worked when we needed some extra money. We were good to go for a while financially since both of our businesses were up and running. Our home was taken care of, and the bills were paid. That was success in my book and meant for a celebration looking back over my childhood because I grew up in poverty. For some reason, he did not feel the same. He was invested and focused only on his business. He could spend days in the office if he could. I did not understand. If it wasn't one thing to worry about it was another. I continued to pray for patience and understanding concerning my husband because it is different to become a new business owner. It was a heavy assignment, but he had me by his side as his helper. I knew his business was very important to him. So, I rolled up my sleeves and asked in what way could I help to alleviate some pressure since I did not have to work double shifts anymore. For a little while everything was good as we ironed out the details of his business. We even combined businesses and finances just to be on the safe side and besides, he was my husband. Therefore, there is no "I" in team. My heart was to partner with him in everything. I had nothing to hide or keep from him, but it seemed like that was not good enough either. I felt like there was no way of pleasing him. Then the arguments started all over again, but this time they were worse. He would say certain things to me that I never thought he would say. It affected my self-esteem and made me look at myself from a different perspective. I didn't realize how much his words had an impact on me. He said he loved me but had crazy unorthodox ways of showing it. I found myself shutting down more and avoiding him because I did not want to make him that upset again. I didn't even know what I was doing to make him so angry. I grew nervous and felt I should just give him space. I was walking on eggshells for some time. I reverted to putting up my guard again because he stepped on many trauma triggers that I thought were buried deep down inside. I even forgot about most of them until he ripped off the bandages and I was exposed and vulnerable again. He eventually made me feel that I was worthless and replaceable to him even as his wife. I didn't know if I should just call it quits because honestly, I was not getting anything from him in return. It had been years since I felt complete and truly loved by him. I asked myself over and over why I should continue to stay only to come up with nothing. I met every need of his and this was the thanks I got in return. I knew I was worthy of love and care, but he did not see it that way. A blind person could see this was a one-sided marriage, but I wanted to continue to love him hoping he would change.

Our home became a hostile environment. I noticed he would act out his past traumatic events on me. It took me by surprise because he never spoke of the abuse he went through unless I was faced with it head-on in an argument. I just assumed he was healthy and able to operate maturely and patiently as I witnessed in the beginning of our relationship. I thought I was the only one with an abusive past that I wanted to escape. Then it hit me. We more than likely only bonded so well because of similar trauma. **Trauma bonds** are emotional bonds that arise from a cyclical pattern of abuse. **Trauma bonding** is a deep emotional attachment that forms between a victim and an abuser within an abusive relationship. It occurs when a person is in a relationship with a narcissist, who often manipulates and exploits their partner's *codependency* issues. Trauma bonds can also form between narcissistic parents and children, who are trained to respond in ways that feed the narcissist's ego and needs. Trauma bonds can create a painful cycle of abuse and dependency that is hard to break.

I didn't realize that my childhood created *codependency* issues. **Codependency** is excessive emotional or psychological reliance on a partner, typically one who requires support on account of an illness, addiction, etc. My husband saw this and took full advantage because he knew I didn't want to be without him. My husband's true character began to unfold, and I had no idea what to expect next. One day I remembered my husband coming into the house late as usual, but he was very angry. He started an argument resulting in him shutting down, ignoring me, and leaving again. Suddenly, my childhood fears came rushing back to me like a storm. I balled up in a corner and felt helpless, abandoned, rejected, and traumatized. Cloud 9 was out of my mind and dreams forever involving my husband. I just knew it would never go back to the way it used to be. Although he repeatedly apologized, I could not fully trust that he wouldn't go back into his normal cycle again. Soon he reminded me of my father. I left Ghana and started a new life to get away only to be brought back full circle. Why didn't I see this in the beginning? I wanted to believe so badly that he was unique and would never do anything to hurt me. He hid his abusive side well. He had me fooled. After constantly going back and forward with him, I fell into depression and had no one else to talk things through. I was in a cage in my mind and couldn't seem to break free no matter how much I fought. Did I make a mistake with marrying this man? A change had to happen quickly because I could not go on another year just coping. Each time I wanted to leave he would do something to make me reconsider and stay. I stayed only to go through the same abuse. If this wasn't a spell I was under, I'm not sure what it was at this point. I had to be sick!

Soon after, I found out I was pregnant and that did not make matters any better. I stayed to myself and only tolerated our marriage for the sake of the baby. The harsh treatment grew, and my partner didn't want anything to do with me most of the time. The cycle of it all was very exhausting. One moment he showed me affection, then the next he hated me and disappeared. He had my mind so confused, but I didn't want our daughter to grow up without a father. So, I tunneled through it most days and on others, I cried myself to sleep. Our daughter was finally born, and I focused all my love and attention on her, so I did not go crazy. She was the ray of joy and peace that I needed to make it through the day. I was so happy to see her face every day. She made waking up to life worth it. If I didn't get anything else out of my marriage, I would've been satisfied with her. I never knew my heart could overflow with joy and gratefulness as I gazed upon her smile. I thought cloud 9 was the dream goal, but the two feelings did not compare to one another. Was this how true love felt? I had never felt this way for my husband or anyone else for that matter.

As I bonded with our daughter, I tried to create a fantasy world where everything was close to perfect, and I had no care in the world. I was determined to pursue happiness every day, but no matter what I did it was not good enough because I still had to deal with the harsh words and lack of empathy from my partner. I began to research therapists in the area, but after a few visits, I didn't have the strength to go anymore. Talking about the trauma repeatedly made me feel dizzy, drained, and uncertain of who I was after a while. I did some research on my own to see if there was anything else out there to help my failing marriage and mind from going crazy. I came across an article that read my partner from A to Z! I knew it had to be a sign to dive in, and so I did. As I read the article, it spoke about people with narcissistic personalities. I had never heard of this type of personality before. This type of personality was getting more and more attention in the media for some reason.

Psychologists have named this sort of person a "narcissist," after Narcissus — someone who has an excessive interest in or admiration of themselves. In Greek mythology, **Narcissus** was a hunter from Thespiae in Boeotia who was known for his beauty which was noticed by all, regardless of gender. According to the best-known version of the story, Narcissus rejected all advances, eventually falling in love with a reflection in a pool of water, tragically not realizing its similarity, entranced by it. In some versions, he beat his breast purple in agony at being kept apart from this reflected love, and in his place sprouted a flower bearing his name. How bizarre is that? This story reminds me of Satan from the Bible who was once known as Lucifer, a very beautiful angel that looked at his reflection in the water too, then pride overtook him. This eventually led him to be kicked out of Heaven and marked for Hell. I could not believe what I was reading because it truly felt like I was living in hell but did not know how to escape.

I started to compare the characteristics of a narcissist to my partner, and it was the same. What I realized is that a narcissist doesn't love anyone because they do not have the mental capacity to do so. They manipulate people to serve as a safe place and to always have somewhere to go back to because they fear getting themselves together and being healed. They know they will have to be responsible for their actions. They use childhood trauma as an excuse for others to pity them as they are adults while they continue the same repeated cycles. You can show them all the love you carry, and they will still make plans to leave just in case something doesn't go their way. They seek attention for power and will never be satisfied. They will mess you up and drain you mentally, physically, and emotionally. A Narcissist is a con artist. They will sell you a dream to deliver you a living nightmare.

According to multiple psychological studies, ***narcissistic personality disorder*** (NPD) is a mental health condition in which people have an unreasonably high sense of their own importance. They need and seek lots of attention and want people to admire them. People with this disorder may lack the ability to understand or care about the feelings of others. But behind this mask of extreme confidence, they are not sure of their self-worth and are easily upset by the slightest criticism. A narcissistic personality disorder causes problems in many areas of life, such as relationships, work, school, or financial matters. People with narcissistic personality disorder may be generally unhappy and disappointed when they're not given the special favors or admiration that they believe they deserve. They may find their relationships troubled and unfulfilling, and other people may not enjoy being around them.

NPD affects more males than females, and it often begins in the teens or early adulthood. Some children may show traits of narcissism, but this is often typical for their age and doesn't mean they'll go on to develop narcissistic personality disorder.

Symptoms of narcissistic personality disorder and how severe they are can vary. People with the disorder can:
- Have an unreasonably high sense of self-importance.
- Require constant and excessive admiration.
- Feel that they deserve privileges and special treatment.
- Expect to be recognized as superior even without achievements.
- Make achievements and talents seem bigger than they are.
- Be preoccupied with fantasies about success, power, brilliance, beauty, or the perfect mate.
- Believe they are superior to others and can only spend time with or be understood by equally special people.
- Be critical of and look down on people they feel are not important.
- Expect special favors and expect other people to do what they want without questioning them.
- Take advantage of others to get what they want.

- Have an inability or unwillingness to recognize the needs and feelings of others.
- Be envious of others and believe others envy them.
- Behave arrogantly, brag a lot, and come across as conceited.
- Insist on having the best of everything — for instance, the best car or office.

At the same time, people with narcissistic personality disorder have trouble handling anything they view as criticism. They can:

- Become impatient or angry when they don't receive special recognition or treatment.
- Have major problems interacting with others and easily feel slighted.
- React with rage or contempt and try to belittle other people to make themselves appear superior.
- Have difficulty managing their emotions and behavior.
- Experience major problems dealing with stress and adapting to change.
- Withdraw from or avoid situations in which they might fail.
- Feel depressed and moody because they fall short of perfection.
- Have secret feelings of insecurity, shame, humiliation, and fear of being exposed as a failure.

When to seek help:

If you are a victim, one of the big signs to leave is when you have to ask yourself the question, "Should I stay, or should I go?"

Children thrive most when their mother is happy. People with narcissistic personality disorder may not want to think that anything could be wrong, so they usually don't seek treatment. If they do seek treatment, it's more likely to be for symptoms of depression, drug or alcohol misuse, or another mental health problem. What they view as insults to self-esteem may make it difficult to accept and follow through with treatment. Treatment for narcissistic personality disorder centers around talk therapy, also called psychotherapy.

You also might benefit from speaking with someone yourself, as loved ones of narcissists often are victims of emotional or physical abuse, gaslighting, and other issues. These are some *signs of narcissistic victim syndrome:*

- *Feelings of Isolation*
- *Self-doubt*
- *Guilt*
- *Difficulties in making decisions*
- *Self-destructive behavior*
- *Loss of self-identity*
- *Inability to set boundaries*
- *Anxiety*
  - *Depression*

Of course, there are so many other symptoms. If you are experiencing these things, seek help. Narcissism is among the issues that plague humans who are slaves to sin and slaves to the flesh. But we can take heart in knowing that Jesus sets the captives free (John 8:34-35). As Believers of Jesus Christ, the Holy Spirit works in us and helps us become better and more like Christ. This process is called sanctification. While we never become perfect, we can become holier, better, and more like Christ over time.

15 Signs You Are Dating a Narcissist

1. They Lack Empathy

Most people can be selfish or struggle to put others before themselves.

Empathy involves the ability to understand and share the feelings of another, to be aware of and be sensitive to the thoughts and experiences of another person. The phrase "put yourself in someone else's shoes" comes to mind — it's the ability to identify with and then, in turn, treat others the way we would want to be treated. However, narcissists are either unable or unwilling to have such empathy for others. They either do not care about someone else's plight or cannot muster the ability to relate to another. Incredibly self-absorbed, they seem not to have any real desire for true, give-and-take emotional intimacy. They want to be heard and understood by another, but they do not offer this in return.

2. A Sense of Entitlement

Many people feel entitled to things in life. Children might feel entitled to new clothing, toys, or cell phones without realizing these are gifts from people who love them. Employees might feel entitled to special perks at the office without realizing this is a kindness their manager offers out of care. A narcissist, however, generally seems to feel like they are entitled to things just because they want them. Often, they expect others to heed their desires. They might get upset if corrected or reprimanded, and they feel they need to be treated as if they are more special, somehow than anyone else. Deep down, they believe they are uncommon, rare, and worthy of so much more than anyone else. They expect the best treatment no matter what, just because. Sometimes, they think the rules don't apply to them and that they are superior to others.

3. They Must Be the Star

Narcissists often don't just want to shine — they feel they need to be the center of attention. If they feel ignored or if someone else gets more attention than they do, they might get unreasonably upset. They seem to crave admiration and constantly fish for compliments and adoration. They want to know what others think of them. Often, this is because deep down, they are plagued with self-doubt, self-criticism, or a pervading sense of emptiness and low self-esteem. Other times, they genuinely have such a high opinion of themselves that they simply believe they are superior to others — deserving of such attention.

They may gossip about people they envy, or make up reasons why that person is successful, attractive, etc. If your loved one is a narcissist, they might desperately crave attention and need to be first or the best. They might feel slighted and filled with envy and anger if they are not. They want to feel appreciated, praised and admired. They crave validation from others.

4. Bragging, Bragging, and More Ragging

Narcissists often brag or exaggerate their accomplishments and come across as arrogant both in behavior and attitude. They may constantly talk about their physical appearance, successes, romantic conquests, or money. They might also talk about how much others flirt with them. They typically see themselves as superior to others and might become rude when they don't receive the treatment, they think they deserve. They may speak or act abusively or rudely, demeaning those they deem to be inferior. They might also overestimate their capabilities or hold themselves to ridiculously high standards. They might also be snobbish or condescending, believing they should associate only with those they see as "worthy." Also, they might use others for their own gain, whether consciously or unconsciously. They might also make friends with people who they believe could increase their status in some way.

5. Exploitation and Manipulation

A narcissist is constantly looking out for their own best interest, thinking of their needs first. Often, they are friends with someone because of what that person can do for them. For example, they marry someone with a good reputation so they can also be seen as good and worthy. They befriend someone who can give them rides to and from places or get them admission to their fancy club or a discount at the store where they work. Often, they use people for their own gain. Narcissists also might try to keep people at a certain distance in order to maintain control over the relationship. "I'll call you," they might say to keep the upper hand. Manipulators often use lies and deceit to control and influence others.

6. They were charming at first

People who have *narcissistic personality disorder* (NPD) gravitate toward grandiosity and fantasy. Your relationship might have felt like a fairytale at first — maybe they complimented you constantly or told you they loved you within the first month. Maybe they tell you how smart you are or emphasize your compatibility, even if you just started seeing each other.

7. They hog the conversation, talking about how great they are

People with NPD can have an inflated sense of self-importance and may exaggerate achievements and expect to be recognized as superior.

8. They feed off your compliments

Narcissists may *seem* super self-confident. But most people with NPD lack self-esteem and require excessive attention and admiration. They need a lot of praise, and if you're not giving it to them, they'll fish for it. That's why they're constantly looking at you to tell them how great they are.

9. They pick on you constantly

Maybe, at first, it felt like teasing, but then it became mean. Suddenly, everything you do, from what you wear and eat to who you hang out with and what you watch on TV, is a problem for them. Antagonism and hostility are well-documented traits in people with NPD, and the toll on others is large. They'll put you down, call you names, hit you with hurtful one-liners, and make jokes that aren't quite funny. Their goal is to lower others' self-esteem so that they can increase their own because it makes them feel powerful. What's more, reacting to what they say may reinforce their behavior. A narcissist loves reactions. That's because it shows them, they have the power to affect another's emotional state. A narcissist makes excuses to make it seem like you had an advantage that they didn't have if you succeed at something. They want you to know that you're not better than them. Because, to them, nobody is.

A warning sign: If they knock you down with insults when you do something worth celebrating, get yourself out of there.

10. They gaslight you

Gaslighting is a form of manipulation and emotional abuse, and it's a hallmark of narcissism. People with NPD may tell blatant lies, falsely accuse others, spin the truth, and ultimately distort your reality — especially in response to perceived challenges of authority or fear of abandonment.

Signs of gaslighting can include:

- You no longer feel like the person you used to be.
- You feel more anxious and less confident than you used to be.
- You often wonder if you're being too sensitive.
- You feel like everything you do is wrong.
- You always think it's your fault when things go wrong.
- You're often apologizing.
- You have a sense that something's wrong but can't identify what it is.
- You often question whether your response to your partner is appropriate.
- You make excuses for your partner's behavior.

Narcissists do this to cause others to doubt themselves to gain superiority. They thrive off being worshipped, so they use manipulation tactics to get you to do just that.

11. They think they're right about everything, and never apologize

People with NPD are often described as being arrogant and having haughty behaviors or attitudes. That's why fighting with a narcissist may feel impossible. There is no debating or compromising with a narcissist because they are always right. They won't necessarily see a disagreement as a disagreement. They'll just see it as them teaching you some truth.

You may be dating a narcissist if you feel like your partner:
- don't hear you
- won't understand you
- doesn't take responsibility for their part in an issue
- don't ever try to compromise
- doesn't think they are ever wrong and will rarely apologize

12. Love Bombing

The action or practice of lavishing someone with attention or affection, especially in order to influence or manipulate them. This is the same tactics cults often use to lure new members. After you are a part of the cult, their true self and mission is revealed and it's not so nice. Love bombing involves showering someone with flattery and attention so that they become deeply attached and want to stay in a relationship regardless of how they are treated. A love bomber aims to isolate their partner from friends and family and become their whole world, leaving them vulnerable to mistreatment. This kind of behavior is a form of emotional abuse, and although it can be experienced during any stage of a relationship, it is often seen in the early stages of getting to know one another. It may seem like your new partner really likes you but love bombing can often serve as a warning sign of an unhealthy relationship. Love bombing most likely is showered upon the victim after an argument or fight so they will not think to leave.

13. Stonewalling

Stonewalling involves refusing to communicate with another person and withdrawing from the conversation to create distance between the individual and their partner. Intentionally shutting down during an argument, also known as "the silent treatment," can be hurtful, frustrating, and harmful to the relationship.

Examples of Stonewalling

- Walking away during an argument

- Giving one- or two-word replies

- Not responding during conversations

- Not showing interest in resolving conflicts

- Silent treatment

- Avoiding eye contact

- Refusal to respond to questions

- Pretending not to notice or hear someone

14. They do not support you

Everything is about them and if your world doesn't revolve around them, it's a problem. Their success is all that matters to them. They distract you from your goals so that you have no choice but to only focus on them. They do not want you to be successful because when they plan their exit, they want you to be left with nothing.

15. When you show them, you're done, they lash out

People with NPD are especially vulnerable to humiliation and shame and tend to lash out at others when they feel their self-esteem has taken a hit. If you insist, you're done with the relationship, they'll make it their goal to hurt you for abandoning them even though they are the problem. Their ego is so severely bruised that it causes them to feel rage and hatred for anyone who 'wronged' them. That's because everything is everyone else's fault. Including the breakup.

While ending the relationship is the best game plan if you're dating or married to someone who has NPD, **avoid negotiation and arguments.** What irritates someone with NPD is the lack of control and the lack of a fight. The less you fight back, the less power you can give them over you, the better. Also, set healthy boundaries and continue to reinforce them if you must have contact with a narcissist for the sake of the children, if apply. If you must converse with a narcissist, keep it short, simple, and to the point. Here are *7 Key phrases to disarm a narcissist:*

- "I can't control how you feel about me."
- "I hear what you are saying."

- "I'm sorry you feel that way."
- "Everything is okay."
- "We both have a right to our own opinions."
- "I can accept how you feel."
- "I don't like how you are speaking to me so I will not engage."

I know it all seems impossible now because of all you have been through, but with determination, consistency, and practice, you can get through this safely. I am living proof that you can get out too!

Healing from a narcissistic relationship can be challenging, but it's essential for your well-being. Here are some steps you can take:

1. **No Contact or Limited Contact**: If possible, **cut off contact** with the narcissist. This includes blocking them on social media, deleting their number, and avoiding places where you might run into them. If you must maintain contact (e.g., co-parenting), keep it **strictly business**.

2. **Seek Professional Help**: Consider **therapy or counseling**. A therapist can help you process your emotions, understand the dynamics of the relationship, and develop coping strategies. **Trauma-focused therapy** can be particularly helpful.

3. **Educate Yourself**: Learn about **narcissism** and its effects. Understand that their behavior is not your fault. Knowledge empowers you to recognize red flags and avoid similar situations in the future.

4. **Self-Care**: Prioritize self-care. **Practice mindfulness**, engage in activities you enjoy, exercise, eat well, and get enough rest. Surround yourself with supportive friends and family. Limit negative inner chatter. Set boundaries with yourself.

5. **Set Boundaries**: Establish clear boundaries with the narcissist. Be assertive about what you will and won't tolerate. Stick to these boundaries even if they try to manipulate or guilt-trip you.

6. **Journaling**: Write down your feelings and experiences. This can help you process emotions and gain clarity.

7. **Rebuild Self-Esteem**: Narcissists often undermine their partners' self-worth. **Affirmations**, positive self-talk, and self-compassion can help rebuild your self-esteem.

8. **Avoid Idealization**: Remember that the charming, idealized version of the narcissist was a facade. Focus on the **reality** of their behavior and the harm they caused.

9. **Support Groups**: Join support groups or online forums where you can connect with others who have experienced narcissistic abuse. Sharing stories and insights can be therapeutic.

10. **Forgive Yourself**: Understand that you were manipulated and deceived. Forgive yourself for any perceived mistakes or shortcomings. Healing takes time.

11. **Cognitive dissonance** is the mental discomfort that results from holding two conflicting beliefs, values, or attitudes. People tend to seek consistency in their attitudes and perceptions, so this conflict causes unpleasant feelings of unease or discomfort. Choose what is right for you.

Remember, healing is a process, and it's okay to seek professional help. You deserve a healthy and fulfilling life beyond the narcissistic relationship.

Chapter 4

The Red Flags

As days went by, the more my husband just couldn't be trusted. We would have conversations, and I would catch him in lies. Then he started staying out all night again. I began to suspect he was cheating, but I had no proof. I was not the type to make accusations about someone. I wanted to come to the table with the facts. Therefore, I waited to gather more information. I had cameras installed throughout our home. I wanted to be able to document the times he was home and the gap of time he spent away. I stayed to myself and did the best I could doing everything alone as a married woman. I knew I had to start considering divorce at some point, but until then I continued to play my role as the wife and mother. Whenever he was home, he always had a meal to eat, clean clothes to wear, and a wife to satisfy his desires. I forced myself to remain intimate with him because I thought we would stay close. I began to find condoms in his things, and he would tell me I was crazy for getting upset because he put them there to use when we didn't want to get pregnant. I could only recall us using condoms a few times and it surely wasn't recent. It became alarming to me when I would repeatedly contract yeast infections and urinary tract infections (UTIs) after we were intimate. There had to be something I was missing, and my body was trying to get my attention. But what? Was he sleeping with someone else, and it was throwing off my PH-balance? I remained submitted to him, but vigilant because he was untrustworthy and lacked empathy for me and our children.

Some time went by, and I thought things would change at least a little. They changed alright!! I found out I was pregnant again and my husband was not so happy. I was in disbelief. I knew I had to brainstorm on an exit plan and figure out how to save money without raising a red flag to my husband, but how now? This pregnancy had my mind gone to another dimension. I could not think straight and lost my appetite for days. I put my exit plans on hold and hoped everything would work out for the better. After all, storms don't last always, right? I continued to have hope that my marriage would become stable for the sake of the children. I wanted my husband to see how much I still loved him and remember how much I had already sacrificed. I didn't know what else to do so I just remained consistent even though I couldn't get that from him. Months flew by and pregnancy took over my body. I needed a break so we agreed that I would stop working and he would upkeep the businesses and bills for our home. I was relieved. The time had come to deliver our son, and my mind was already on the future. I wanted to know what life would be like after our son came home. Once we were discharged, my husband was very nice for the first few days. After that, he would disappear for weeks at a time and when he was home, we would argue like cats and dogs. I knew something was different, but I couldn't put my finger on it.

I remember him popping up at the house to retrieve Amazon packages periodically, then disappearing again. A few times the packages would be shipped before he got to the house, so I opened them out of curiosity, and it was always things for a woman. I asked him about the packages, and he would say he was buying gifts for his sister and to stay out of his business. I asked him to show me our financial records because some of those gifts looked very expensive. He refused and told me I was crazy and overreacting. When we agreed for me to stop working, my husband said that it would help us financially if everything went into his name. So, I agreed since he said he mapped out a way for us to gain more money. He oversaw everything we had, the money, the businesses, etc. I wanted to trust that he would do the right thing, especially for our children. I went back to work, but shortly after that, I lost my job due to the pandemic. I filed for unemployment and was denied. When they told me I was not eligible because I hadn't filed a tax return in years, I immediately became furious! I knew this was all my husband's doing because he had a track record of doing sneaky things, but I never thought he would not file me on our taxes. I thought my husband was filing taxes all this time with us as a joint status, but he only filed for himself and did not share any of this with me. I visited his business to question him, but he had just stepped out. The secretary was there so I began to question her about the financial records. I had no idea if she had access to them or not but turns out she did. The financial records showed me everything I needed to know. My husband locked me out of everything so that I would no longer have access to our money or businesses.

The secretary then told me she signed for my husband a new apartment. An apartment? I was confused and did not know how to receive her statement since I was already in a whirlwind after getting denied unemployment. I wasn't even sure why she was so open with me about it. I knew of her but didn't know too much about her. It was like I just looked up one day and she was there. I didn't argue about it because my husband said he needed help. I tried to help, but I guess after our first child was born, he assumed I would've had no time to be there for his business. Why did she even share news about an apartment? Why did she need to sign for it? What did he need an apartment for anyway? I went into the office I had inside his building and grabbed as many important things as I could. I'm not sure why, but I felt a tug to get my belongings out of the office, so I did. I couldn't get everything though so I packed the car with what I could get. I figured I had time to make another trip later. The secretary just looked at me crazy and got back to work. I didn't put it all together at that moment. I needed to leave to catch my breath and clear my mind. I cried all the way home because so many emotions hit me at once. My mind was all over the place.

Was it finally over and he was moving out of the house? How could the man I helped to build up from the ground, do these surprisingly horrible things to me? I felt as if I didn't even know him anymore. I thought we would build to become a power couple and take our children further than our parents took us. Turns out he just used me as a stepping stool to get what he wanted and to succeed in life. It never was about me or our children. He only wanted to secure his future, and I was the pawn in his game. How could I be so stupid and blind not to see his plans from the beginning? I guess love really will blind you if you do not pair it with the wisdom of God. He took everything away from me and our children after my name was no longer on anything. The money, future family goals, medical insurance, house, ways to get food, etc. were all gone! All I had was the little money in my savings account and that dried up quickly because I was always tapping into it to help him in the beginning of our marriage. He also took my self-worth, dignity, and pride. I had no clue who I was anymore or how I would pick up the pieces with two children.

I'm sure the secretary told him I visited the office because he blocked my calls and locked me out of the building by changing all the locks. He didn't reach out to me until days later when he found out I was in the emergency room with the kids! I remember having to rush the kids to the hospital without medical insurance. I had no idea how I was going to pay for the upfront cost, so I called my husband many times that day for help. I'm sure he only called me back because he was afraid Child Protective Services would get involved if the children couldn't be seen and treated due to lack of money. I found myself having to beg him for money and this was my breaking point. I tried to hold onto my idea of "family" as long as I could, but once our children's lives were put in jeopardy, I couldn't compromise anymore with my husband. Our children didn't ask to be born and deserved to be properly taken care of by both parents. If he ran off with all our money, how was I to afford to care for our children? He would even disappear for weeks without communication or paying his portion of the bills. I contributed financially until my husband took full control of all our money once I had our first child. I realized that I lost my value in my husband's eyes after I got pregnant. I would cry myself to sleep after putting the kids to bed because I knew we would never be a complete and healthy family.

I felt my life crumble before my very eyes. I knew it was time to file for divorce and take everything back that he stole from me for the sake of our children's survival. He betrayed me to the highest degree! Even through the abuse and disrespect, I did right by him because he was my husband, and this was what my life became. I got tired of pretending that everything was fine and that was far from the truth. I filed for divorce and was sure I was making the right choice. I had to take out a loan just to pay the lawyer fees. As the lawyer began to form the case, I got cold feet and wondered if I was overreacting. I had faith that the lawyer would get me and the kids everything we needed to survive, but I was so scared to face my husband after the papers were served so I backed out. All the lawyer fees I paid upfront were non-refundable, and the lawyer was upset with me for not going through with the divorce. I knew I didn't want to stay in a failed and abusive marriage. Therefore, I was upset with myself, but everything was moving too fast. Maybe I didn't think everything through and needed more time. The lawyer wanted the best for me and the kids. He knew I needed to leave the marriage after hearing my case, but it was completely my call if I wanted to proceed. I don't know what happened! Fear gripped me and I couldn't shake it. I was a victim on so many levels and could not get out of my head. I figured if I did some research to find common ground with my husband, he wouldn't be angry with me, and the kids wouldn't get hurt. All research pointed me to either get a divorce or to stay wrapped up in *domestic violence*. What did they mean by domestic violence? I knew I was facing abuse, but I didn't think it was classified as domestic violence because I had no physical scars like my mom did when I was younger. I then realized my fear came from other forms of domestic violence over time that I had no idea existed. I read and heard about domestic violence in other people's relationships, but I never thought it would happen to me. Many think it's only fighting and leaving with horrendous physical scars, or it wouldn't be classified as a domestic violence case. I was so beaten down mentally, verbally, and emotionally that I couldn't identify myself even while looking in the mirror. I just wanted to be able to provide for our children, but I knew I had to be free from fear and face my husband.

Domestic Violence

Domestic violence (also known as family violence) is when someone uses violence or manipulation to maintain power and control over someone they're close to. It can involve violence, intimidation, threats, insults, or psychological manipulation. Domestic violence is usually a pattern of abusive and controlling behavior taking many forms, and it happens in intimate, family, or informal care relationships. The United States Department of Justice defines domestic violence as "a pattern of abusive behavior in any relationship that is used by one partner to gain or maintain control over another intimate partner." The term "domestic violence" is used when there is a close relationship between the offender and the victim. Domestic violence is similar to covert abuse. *Covert abuse* can be defined as abuse that is kept hidden or is not acknowledged. This type of abuse may be physical as is the case when someone abuses an individual in a way that is not readily seen (leaving bruises in places covered by clothes for example), or it may be verbal, emotional, or mental.

The Financial Abuse

Financial abuse is a form of domestic abuse and is a way of having power over another. It involves someone else controlling your spending or access to cash, assets, and finances. Financial abuse can prevent you from working, restrict or steal your own money, or misuse or pressure you regarding your money or property. This type of abuse can make you feel isolated, lacking in confidence, and trapped.

My husband controlled all my spending claiming he was just trying to help us maintain our wealth. For everything I needed, I had to ask his permission and wait until he gave me the money for it. As I already stated, I was locked out of all our financial records and accounts although I was the owner of our businesses as well. Even when it came to making decisions for our businesses, I was left out and not told anything. I had to find out through others if a crisis was happening in the business. I was constantly belittled and made to feel like I was nothing. My achievements, hard work, and sacrifice for our success were quickly forgotten. He made me feel as if I didn't play a major part in the building process or make any sacrifices for our future. My husband also closed all my financial accounts and removed my name from the deed of the home we purchased, so if I left, I would walk away with nothing. Although, staying I had nothing. I didn't know which was worse. He would threaten to have me removed from the house every day and even refused to give me money to support the kids. I know I was blind and allowed him to gain too much power over me, but if I had foreseen all of this, I would've made better choices. In the beginning, I wanted to trust him because he was my husband, and we took vows. Plus, we had two wonderful children together.

Having been denied finances for so long, left me trying to frantically pick up the broken pieces of my life. I had to do it for the kids. I decided to start a new business. Although I felt crazy, I knew I could do it because I already did it before. Where would I get the start-up money? I had to clear my mind and think. How hard could it be, right? There were many times I wondered if I would ever overcome this storm of my life. Would I even make enough in my new business to provide for the children and myself? Giving up wasn't an option for me. I kept striving and found ways to make passive income without having to work a regular 9-5 job. I wanted to be able to be there for my children.

The Impact of Financial Abuse

I had taken a huge loss even before I realized I was being financially abused and used. Shortly after my husband took full control of all our income, he stopped paying the bills concerning our home. Little did I know he was sending money to Ghana so that he could build mansions there for his family and ministry. He even got a new apartment with his mistress behind my back and made sure the bills there where paid. I sacrificed over ten years of my life, time, money, etc. to help my husband become successful and ended up with the short end of the stick. My credit score even dropped tremendously because I put everything I needed to pay off at the bottom of the list, so my husband's goals were met. My credit score became so low that I couldn't get anything else in my name after a while. Everything I had was poured into my husband's business and I soon forgot all about my needs because I loved him that much. I wanted to see him happy, and I wanted us to live a comfortable life. That's what a wife does, right? In the past, he even convinced me to invest in an organization that turned out to be no good for us, but I trusted him telling me everything was going to be alright. I ended up losing lots of money from my savings. Hence why I barely have any left to survive on now. The organization we invested in had a secret agenda that I knew nothing about, but I feel my husband knew their agenda. It was a devastating disaster to lose so much of my savings! I should've known then that he was only concerned about his wellbeing. I quickly exited the contract of the investment deal before I lost more money and had to slowly rebuild while my husband didn't even lose sleep over it.

I always wondered if my husband got money out of the deal and just didn't share it with me. Then to experience years later my husband stealing all the money we made together and locking me out of everything made me feel like a fool for trusting him. It forced me to start over, this time from the bottom with two children depending on me alone. I was overwhelmed, depressed, sometimes suicidal, bitter, angry, resentful, etc. I experienced a monsoon of emotions that I could barely control, but I got through it with the help of God. I realized being financially independent and using wisdom helps women avoid the dangers of being financially abused, taken advantage of, or easily manipulated. Therefore, hold on to your power and do not trust everyone. They should earn your trust. Do not look past the red flags!

The Fear and The Threats

I decided to officially file for divorce again because our marriage was a lost cause. I had to go through with it all the way, no more backing out! I knew there was nothing I could do to change our marriage. I was tired of living in constant fear wondering what he would do next. I worked from home and found myself checking our perimeter cameras all the time. I went into isolation because I did not know who to trust since we shared a lot of friends and associates. I remember having to turn down lots of invites to events of mutual friends because I did not want to run into my husband. I would end up just sending a gift and card explaining that I couldn't make the party. Our friends never made a big deal about it and were kind for the most part. I was relieved that they didn't question me, but I was saddened by the shift that had to take place. I eventually expressed a few details about my situation to one friend because I trusted him to keep quiet. Then I received an invitation to his surprise birthday party and planned to attend. Once I arrived, I saw that he invited my husband too! I felt offended and called the so-called friend out on being inconsiderate of my situation. He knew I couldn't stand to be in the same room at that time with the man who was trying to ruin my life. I panicked and all I could think about was leaving the party immediately once I saw my husband. So many emotions weighed in on my heart that I had to have a seat and take a deep breath. Anger was at the top of my emotions, but I knew that was not my character.

Therefore, I had to calm myself down because no person should have that much control over another to make them act out of character. When my husband saw me, his show began. He made sure he spoke loudly so I wouldn't miss him, and he started mingling all over the room. The room was his stage, and I was the rug he trampled on. He smiled the whole time as if everything was going great in his life and serenaded the crowd non-stop. He had to be the center of attention, or it just wouldn't be right. Everyone fell in love with him and his jokes even more. I was so disgusted! Finally, when I couldn't stomach it anymore, I left the party graciously. I could not get away fast enough! Once I left, the so-called friend was upset that I didn't stay and ridiculed me for living in fear. I expressed all of this before I was even invited to the party. Therefore, I did not feel bad about leaving the celebration early. I did feel set up and not sure whose side my friend was on. So, I just stayed to myself as I went through the wicked process of divorce.

The Impact of Divorce on the Children

As the divorce began to unfold, our children were impacted harshly. After most divorces the man will not only leave the wife but leave the children too. During our divorce our children did not understand what was going on because they were young, and I did not want to share a lot of details with them. I felt kids should not have to witness certain things in life and relationship issues were one. I didn't want them to hate their father based on what I was going through with him. I wanted them to form their own opinions about him when the time was right, and they were old enough to understand some things. I knew I did not get points for speaking badly about their father to them. I respected those boundaries and wanted the same in return from my soon-to-be ex-husband.

Therefore, I covered up lots of things that were going on in and out of court, but no matter how good I was at it, the children still had questions. They wanted to know when Dad was coming back home and when we would take family trips again. Eventually, I had to tell them he wasn't coming back, and they would soon be able to visit him. I left it at that unless they had more questions, but our daughter did not take it well. I noticed she had stopped eating as much, but I didn't want to pressure her into eating. I know sometimes people stop eating when they are trying to sort through a crowd of emotions at once. I wanted to give her that space but always assured her I was there just in case she wanted to talk. She insisted on being alone so I would just check on her from time to time.

It wasn't until I realized she had lost so much weight, and her clothes weren't fitting properly that something had to be done. I asked her over and over if she wanted to talk, but I guess she didn't know how to form her feelings into words. She finally came clean and told me she was throwing up the little food that she ate throughout the day. I couldn't believe our daughter was doing the things I had only seen in movies. Our daughter's behavior humbled me, and I had to let go of the pride I carried due to the divorce process to be able to reach her. I took her to see a doctor and they wanted to run labs on her to make sure it wasn't a physical sickness that took over her body. The results came back showing that her iron and vitamin levels were extremely low, and she was malnourished. She had even lost 40 pounds within weeks. I told the doctor what was going on and they told me that the rate our daughter was going was unhealthy and she could die from starvation.

I became worried and didn't know what to do. I cried uncontrollably trying to settle my mind. Our daughter was punishing her body because of the pain she felt when her dad left and stopped calling. She was also trying to cope knowing my husband and I fought through the divorce process. I knew there would be things to deal with as the divorce continued, but I never thought our daughter would be near death. I wanted to give up, but the only way we could try to get back to a somewhat normal life was if the divorce was quickly finalized. Due to an ongoing project, I had in Ghana, most of my money and resources were exhausted. Therefore, it took me longer to pay off the lawyer's retainer fee to complete everything. I still did not give up! I compared all my options before filing the paperwork again and I was determined to see it through this time. There was nothing left to hold onto anymore. It was the best thing to do for us all, especially since my husband moved out and turned his back on me and the kids. He didn't want to be married or father our children anymore. He made it clear after he expressed that what we had was not a marriage and I found out he had been cheating with his secretary for years. That was why she bought the apartment for him. They wanted to be together without restrictions. It all made sense. I had to be alright with starting over, but never thought it would be at the expense of our daughter taking it as hard as she did. She even struggled with anger and anxiety after a while.

I didn't know what else to do, so I reached out to her school counselor and told them about her situation. I was advised to get her mental help and outside support, so I did. Our daughter was assigned a counselor, and it was the best thing for her. After just a few sessions, she understood what she was going through was a serious matter and could result in death. She began to eat more and decided not to throw up her food anymore. I even noticed a tremendous change in her behavior. Many times, children will listen to their parent's advice and not consider it, but when a stranger says the same thing, it suddenly makes sense to them. I'm not sure why that happens. I guess some kids just need to see for themselves. I was ready and willing to do whatever had to be done to help our daughter get better. I was so grateful because I'm not sure what I would've done if we lost her. Although she still has her moments of fighting the process, she makes progress every day. We continue to work through it with the help of God and therapy where she releases built-up emotions and thoughts.

The Hoovering

Hoovering is an abuse tactic frequently used by people who struggle with narcissistic, borderline, antisocial, and histrionic personality disorders. It is named after the Hoover vacuum cleaner.

Hoovering is used to suck a partner —or ex-partner — back into a situation, conversation, or even a relationship that is toxic, abusive, or unsafe. It is most often deployed when the narcissist fears the partner is moving away or has gained personal empowerment.

7 Facts to Know About Hoovering

1. Hoovering is not about their love for you. They want attention.
2. Responding to a hoover doesn't mean a narcissist will engage with you. Their need for attention was just met.
3. Block them! They will continue to contact you just to see how they can feed off you.
4. You don't want to be hoovered. Hoovering can appear to be love and compassion, but it's just a plan to get you back into their hold.
5. Notice their apology isn't an apology. Narcissists never take responsibility for their actions, but they don't want you to realize that.
6. They're trying to avoid feelings of guilt and shame. They will do anything to avoid facing themselves or what they've done to you.
7. Consider how much more peaceful your life is without them. Close the door and do not give in to their empty words and broken promises.

As the divorce continued, my husband and I argued like crazy. I thought he would at some point have enough time to think and just come home, but he stood strongly on his decision to move on. He told me I was crazy for even thinking we had a marriage from the start. I was so heartbroken to know what we had was never real. I was the only one giving 100% while he just profited from me. I cried so much one night just thinking about all the years I threw away with him. I felt like I was hit by a truck. He just walked away with no care in the world. I guess when he realized I was going through with the divorce process this time, he started coming around the house once a week to see the kids for a few hours at a time. I knew he was doing this on purpose because he knew I no longer wanted to share the same space with him, but the kids wanted to see him. Therefore, I was stuck in the middle trying to be fair. I would go in the other room while he was there, but he still found a way to follow me to say random disrespectful things about the divorce. I had a hard time reading him. One minute he had me to believe he was changing his mind to come back home and the next minute his toxic behavior would raise its ugly head, and I would grow afraid of him again. I didn't want the kids to think I was making it difficult for them to see their father, but I couldn't continue to play his games. I had to set boundaries to protect myself. I was going through with the divorce no matter what but, I did not want to "rock the boat" too much. I knew of the wickedness in his heart and the anger he harbored toward me. I tried my best to keep the peace. I had to live for our children.

The Silent Treatment

Silent Treatment is a kind of abuse that tells someone that I am going to punish you but does not acknowledge your existence. It's an act of withholding communication. The silent treatment is a common stonewalling tactic and can be intentional or unintentional. Some use it as a coping mechanism and others use it to cause harm to the next. When used for harm, the person usually makes the victim feel as if they are the problem by denying the silent treatment altogether. This is also a form of manipulation and gaslighting.

Ways to overcome hostile silent treatment:
1. Avoid becoming isolated.
2. Maintain a rich inner life such as hobbies, etc.
3. Remember yourself and practice self-care.
4. Decide what your limits are and stick to the boundaries.
5. Consider ending the relationship.

Many times, in our relationship, my husband would use the silent treatment to silence me and to push me away. He kept me out of important business decisions and life events including but not limited to his college graduation, coronation, projects he had done in Ghana, his involvement with his relatives, etc. Every time he had something big planned, he would start an argument with me and then shut down once he baited me in. He would go silent for weeks at a time. He even made excuses for the silent treatment by blaming me for doing things he didn't agree with, like helping my now elderly parents back in Ghana. I knew he could care less about the times I helped my parents after I found out through social media that he built his grandmother a house and helped his sister start her business unbeknown to me. He just needed to find a way to close me out of parts of his life as if we weren't even married. Our mutual friends even knew of his plans while I had to play as a detective on social media to find things out. He would give me the silent treatment so much that it felt like we divorced long before I filed the papers. The day I realized he just up and moved out, made me look back on all the times I faithfully stayed through this abuse. It was all in vain because his mind was made up from the beginning that he would use me and then leave. My heart was broken into many pieces. I felt betrayed. I spent so much energy and time trying to keep a man who didn't want to be kept.

I had to work on letting go of the anger towards him. I had too much at stake. My desire and goal were to raise healthy children even though they were a product of a broken marriage. I know God kept us through it all. I believe the divorce was a blessing in disguise to help us heal and gain peace as a family. I could not stay another day with a man who did not have a desire for intimacy with me, converse, or share his dreams and visions with me. I hated the silent treatment he gave me if I disagreed with him concerning any topic. My opinions never mattered to him. He was trying to train me to always agree with him just so I could consider the few words he gave to me an award. He didn't know how to love me the way I deserved to be loved as a wife and as a person who deserves love. I'm someone who loves greatly and deeply. He took advantage of my vulnerability and that I craved partnership. I have faith that God will send the one He has for me. I keep hope for the future of my children, although fear tries to consume my mind sometimes. I keep my relationship with God alive because I believe this is the only thing that keeps me sane.

Fear Shocked

I noticed over time that he became very impulsive which would look like a mid-life crisis to some. He would buy many cars, constantly change his hairstyles and fashion, look overly sexy when he traveled, etc. One day he asked if he could pick up the kids for a few hours and I agreed just to keep the peace. Once the kids returned, our son couldn't wait to tell me about the new "toys" their dad brought. I asked him to share, and he whispered, "Daddy has three guns," as if it was a secret. My heart immediately sank to my feet. I did not know what to say after that or what to think. Why did he take our children with him to buy guns? Why did he suddenly need guns? Fear took over my body! I knew the divorce was pressing some buttons for him and stirring up animosity, but would he plan to kill me? I had many thoughts in the past of dying at his hand because of the abuse and now everything was looking clear. I quickly reached out to the divorce lawyer to recommend to me an advocate concerning his visitation rights. I did not think it was even safe for the children to visit him. I felt so violated knowing my innocent babies were exposed to their father's compulsive behavior. The following week he did not even call to check on the kids, just silence. I was kind of relieved, but I hated that the children had to get used to his broken promises and inconsistencies. I felt so helpless and frustrated that I could not protect them in the areas their dad fell short. I was subject to the court's rules that didn't always have the best interest of the children. I felt as if I was stuck until all the court proceedings were complete. Life events hit differently when children are involved, but I had to continue to remind myself that everything will work out for the best. I had to keep fighting and not give up.

The Outside Dynamics of Divorce/ Flying Monkeys

Very few people knew we were going through a divorce because we chose to keep that private for the sake of the children. Mutual friends had questions about our relationship, but they never came out to ask. I could tell some were concerned by the way they would handle us in passing. I even noticed how most of them would invite him to big events and leave me out. I wouldn't even find out until the events were over. They always held him in the highest esteem for whatever reason. Therefore, if they knew about us splitting, they would side with him. Most times I was treated just as his wife without a name. I felt invisible sometimes and wondered why no one had seen the angry and abusive side of my husband that my children and I knew. I didn't want to expose him. I just wanted him to change. It was a hard pill to swallow, but I continued to love and walk in grace.

Some days were easier than others when it came to my connection with my husband. People would come up to me all the time and tell me my husband was amazing. It would make me so angry inside because I knew it was just a front to capture the hearts of people for praise. Behind the scenes, this was not his life. He was a hypocrite, and I hated it. He dropped the ball on his first ministry which is his family. The people would rain compliments upon him as if he were their god! It was always "Your husband is so generous and kind," "Your husband is so handsome and amazing." They would praise him for his work in the ministry of helping the homeless and feeding those in need. He would even do random things like walk into a Starbucks and pay for everyone's order in line all for attention. I knew his heart was wicked, so it was not out of the kindness of his heart. He craved praise and attention everywhere he went. People would play right into his hands seeing all the glitz and glam and desire a connection to him. I even had friends turn on me just to keep their connection safe with my husband. It was like he had a spell on people that laid eyes on him. All he needed was one glance and he got them just like he got me in the beginning. Every time I looked over our relationship, I asked myself how Satan crept into my life without me even noticing it. I realized when there are open doors of unresolved issues in one's life, the doors give access to things and people who are not there for your best interest. I was blinded by childhood trauma and ended up with someone who sold me the dream I desired. Healing is so important. It's the key to a bright future.

Culture Implications

"Cultural implications" refers to the idea that certain actions and items can have different implications depending on the culture in which they occur. Essentially, the context for seemingly "regular" things can change significantly because different cultures interpret them differently. Culture, society, and religion are the three main avenues that mold one's belief and perspective of the world. Also, famous sayings such as, "They all cheat, so I might as well stay in the relationship," limit one's mindset, morals, and values.

1. **Health and Culture**:
   - Cultural behaviors have significant implications for human health. Culture, which encompasses socially transmitted knowledge, beliefs, and practices, varies across groups and individuals. It has been a critical mode of adaptation throughout human history.

   - **Importance**: Socioeconomic status, gender, religion, and moral values all influence how individuals experience, conceptualize, and react to their world. A general understanding of cultural groups is insufficient for grasping a patient's unique experience with health and illnesses.

- o **Holistic Care**: Healthcare providers can improve individual outcomes by considering an individual's cultural experience and social pressures.

2. **Cultural Influences on Behavior and Decision-Making**:
    - o **Brain Wiring**: Culture provides a framework for behavioral and affective norms. Studies in cultural psychology reveal differences and similarities across populations in behavior, cognition, and emotion.

    - o **Key to Relationships**: Understanding cultural influences is essential for developing meaningful relationships, gaining perspective, and making informed decisions.

Cultural context significantly shapes our perceptions, behaviors, and interactions. Therefore, culture has a big impact on the way people live their lives. In different cultures, the same nonverbal gestures can convey vastly different meanings. Here are a few examples of cultural implications related to **nonverbal communication/gestures** just to paint the picture for you:

1. **Hand Gestures**:

   o **Thumbs Up**: In Western cultures (such as the United States), a thumbs-up gesture typically signifies approval or agreement. However, in some Middle Eastern countries (like Iran), it can be offensive and equivalent to showing the middle finger.

   o **"OK" Sign**: Forming a circle with the thumb and index finger is commonly used to indicate "okay" or "good" in Western cultures. Yet, in Brazil, Germany, and parts of the Middle East, it can be interpreted as vulgar or offensive.

   o **Beckoning Gesture**: In Western cultures, we often beckon someone by extending the arm and curling the index finger toward us. However, in some Asian cultures (such as Japan), this gesture is considered impolite. Instead, they use an open hand, palm down, to signal someone to come closer.

2. **Personal Space**:

   o **Proxemics**: The concept of personal space varies across cultures. In crowded cities like Tokyo, people are accustomed to standing close to each other on trains and sidewalks. In contrast, in Scandinavian countries, people maintain a larger personal space bubble.

- o **Greeting Distance**: When meeting someone for the first time, the appropriate distance for a handshake or a hug differs. Some cultures prefer a warm embrace, while others opt for a more reserved handshake.

3. **Eye Contact**:
   - o **High vs. Low Eye Contact**: In Western cultures, direct eye contact is often seen as a sign of confidence and honesty. However, in some Asian cultures (e.g., Japan), prolonged eye contact can be considered impolite or confrontational. Maintaining a lower gaze is respectful.

   - o **Gender Differences**: In some cultures, men and women have different norms regarding eye contact. For instance, in some Middle Eastern cultures, men avoid prolonged eye contact with women to show respect.

Of course, cultural implications extend beyond these examples and touch every aspect of human behavior, from communication to social norms, rituals, and values. When you are a married woman from Ghana as I am, certain things are forbidden like divorce. My mother and father went through a lot of tribulations in their marriage, but it would've been frowned upon if my mother wanted to leave. In Ghana, women have fewer resources extended to them than men and they barely have a voice when it comes to most topics.

Women have rights in Ghana, but gender equality is still an uphill battle. Therefore, if my father wanted to leave my mother, it would not have been a big deal due to the practice of polygamy. Men are entitled to multiple wives whereas women are not. In Ghana, men can get away with a lot of things that women cannot. Women have fought for many years to gain equality, but the fight continues to this day.

Once I thought about divorce, I was afraid of what others would think of me. In my culture, abuse or a toxic marriage was not a good enough reason to leave my husband because that was the norm for most households. Hence why I stayed so long in my toxic marriage until I just couldn't deal with it anymore. Crimes against women such as rape, domestic violence, and genital mutilation are overlooked on purpose in my culture to keep women quiet and submitted to men. Therefore, women have lived in fear for years trying to figure out a way to be free. In Ghana, most families arrange marriages for their young daughters and pay a dowry to the man who will marry them to be sure the deal is sealed. Marriage is more of a business deal to keep both families out of poverty. Most women do not marry for love. They do it out of submission to their father. Otherwise, the family would turn their back on the woman, and she would be forced to work and care for herself. So, women choose marriage over working because women do not get paid nearly as much as men and they would live in poverty for the rest of their days. Women go into marriages with the mindset of becoming slaves or property just to get by in life. When it comes to relationships in Ghana, cultural nuances play a significant role. Understanding the cultural context can enhance or break your marriage.

1. **Family Involvement:**
   - Ghanaian culture places a strong emphasis on family bonds. Family approval is often crucial in marriage. Expect to be introduced to your partner's family early on, and building a positive rapport with them is essential.
   - Extended family members are also important, and maintaining good relationships with them matters.

2. **Social Expectations:**
   - Social norms and expectations significantly influence dating practices. Most Ghanaians do not adapt to other cultures well because they take pride in their own. Traditional gender roles may impact relationship dynamics as well.
   - Most Ghanaian men are often known for their **strong sense of commitment** in relationships. They approach relationships with seriousness and a long-term perspective. They do not practice divorce but will introduce other options into their lives.

3. **Communication and Respect:**
   - Show respect, especially for elders and men. Respect for religious beliefs and spirituality is also crucial.

Once I decided to step outside the cultural expectations and norms, I was faced with all types of persecution. Many would say my marriage ended because I was too educated, didn't work hard enough to fix his mess, didn't keep him happy, didn't overlook the "norm" of cheating, wasn't submissive enough, etc. I was fed up with everyone blaming me for what my husband did or failed to do in our marriage. The naysayers tried to take my voice away just as my husband did, but today I stand by my decision of divorce and do not regret it. Culture can be a wonderful thing as long as it's not at the expense of abusing someone. I love being from Ghana, but I do pray many things will change for the better especially gender equality.

The Dissociative Phase

Dissociation encompasses the **feeling of daydreaming or being intensely focused,** as well as the distressing experience of being disconnected from reality. In this state, consciousness, identity, memory, and perception are no longer naturally integrated.

As the divorce proceedings were going forward, I remember finding myself daydreaming about a perfect life back with my husband. Of course, I didn't want to break up our family. I just wanted him to change back into the man I first met. He was charming, caring, kind, and communicated everything with me. He included me in his world, and I felt he truly loved me, and I held a special place in his life. Hence why I was willing to go to the ends of the world for him until I saw he was selfish and just taking advantage of me. I had dissociative moments where I longed for him to come back home and apologize, so we could live happily ever after. I was even willing to forgive him for everything he had done to me and the kids just to keep our family together. I would fantasize daily about the perfect life with my husband, hoping I would wake up and the toxic marriage and divorce proceedings were just a dream. The church I even attended frowned upon divorce and continually convinced me to stay with my husband. They did not believe people should get divorced because someone cheated. They told me to fast, pray harder, and to love my husband through it. The church leaders told me that love can change things, but I had a hard time believing that because the marriage was killing me inside after a while.

Unfortunately, I had to realize that my life took an unexpected turn, and I could not control someone else's behavior. We both made a choice, and I must live with that for the rest of my life. I did all I could do and now must live for my children until God sends someone who is truly for me. I was scared every step that I took, so if I did it, so can you!

Chapter 5

Shifting My Pain into Resilience

After all the doing was done, I had to focus on living a new life without my husband. I never pictured life as someone who was divorced because in my country divorce is frowned upon and viewed as a failure. It took me some time, but I got to the point that my marriage was a thing of the past. I took self-care more seriously and even introduced my children to self-care especially after what our oldest child endured through the divorce process. It was time to live on purpose instead of existing in the shadows. I had to forgive and release all the anger, shame, and guilt. I realized only God could change people and it was not my responsibility to take ownership of my husband's actions. I had to deal with my wrongs and do better.

"Do the best you can until you know better. Then when you know better, do better."

-Maya Angelou

I was willing to do any and everything to move on and let the past be the past. I had to accept my portion of accountability for all the baggage I chose to carry around instead of letting it go. I even gave the trauma, pain, and hurt to God so He could heal the scars and wounds that were infected. I could no longer blame my husband for a lot of things because I could have left sooner. He did not force me to stay. I chose to stay thinking my presence and love could change my husband and make our marriage work. I felt helpless many times in my marriage, but I was the one who overlooked the red flags and gave my power away.

I have learned to lean into my emotions and deal with them head-on. I fear that the moments will overtake me sometimes, but I chose to clear my mind and dive in. This has been a journey for me, and I try not to compare my process with anyone else's because I know that would more than likely set me back. I have decided to do things to keep me levelheaded and remain strong for my children. I have started writing or journaling, which I am doing right now at 1:00 am while everyone in the house is asleep. I also started a podcast and YouTube channel that brings more awareness to mental health, although sometimes I am afraid to post certain videos because of the fear of what others would say. I am working on leaving the fear and the perfectionist mindset behind. I like to lift weights, stretch, and meditate on God's Word. Self-care and spiritual care are important because you cannot have one without the other. At the end of the day, God has the final say concerning the matter. He created us all with a purpose and a destiny, but it's up to us to seek Him for the path and plan. I have also built my finances back up so that me and my children could be stable again without having to beg for money. My goal was to partake in passive streams of income so that I could spend the maximum amount of time with my children, and I succeeded because I never gave up. When I feel the overwhelming sensation of stress trying to drag me back to the past, I engage in therapy sessions to release everything without feeling guilty or judged. I am building my wings stronger each day so that I can fly higher in my decision-making capabilities.

Five years from now my prayer is to host more domestic violence groups for women so they too can have a safe place to voice their thoughts. I want to be able to give them tools to help them make the right decisions. I also hope my medical practice will take off so that more people dealing with mental health issues will be able to discover and select safer and natural treatments. My practice focuses on a holistic approach that is natural and almost eliminates side effects that traditional medicines would give. I focus on the overall mind, body, soul, and spirit of the person. All things are connected, and it would take longer to heal if all areas were not addressed at some point. My main goal is to bring the healthiest version of YOU to the surface. In my five-year goal, I would like to get remarried to the right man if it's God's will for my life. God would truly have to send the next man to my doorstep because I do not want to make the same mistakes of trying to choose my purpose or destiny again. I have learned my lesson and now it is time to grow beyond it. I use the power that God has given me so I can unlock the things from Heaven that I need to fulfill my God-given purpose.

"I can do all things through Christ which strengthened me."
Philippians 4:13 KJV

In conclusion, I hope that after reading this book it gives you more confidence to take a stand. Each relationship or situation is different and only you can determine when you have had enough. Marriage is not a "one size fits all" fix. Evaluate your likes and dislikes. What makes you happy? What can you tolerate? Set healthy boundaries and be serious about them. Make yourself a priority because if you don't, no one else will. Yes, God wants us to love others, but rest in the full understanding that we love others as we love ourselves. Loving ourselves is just as important. We teach people how to treat us based on how we treat ourselves and what we tolerate. Set your standards high and do not settle. The right person for you will line up. If they leave you, they were not for you and that is okay. Understanding that will save you a lot of stress, heartache, and heartbreak.

Fear will try to creep in but take a stand anyway. God will help you to navigate and get into the right alignment. Embrace fearlessness, happiness, joy, peace, and gratitude. Gratitude is the quality of being thankful; and readiness to show appreciation for and to return kindness. Gratitude drive purpose and it helps you to live a balanced life. We all strive for happy, sunny days, but know that storms, rain, and disappointments will happen. It is up to us to see the good in everything and hold on tight as if our lives depend on it.

I also could not smoothly transition to the healthy version of myself if I did not have a supportive village. Although my circle of friends, family, and church family is small, I needed them when the times got foggy, and I could not see my way. They served as a light in the caves or tunnels where I found myself standing still. I thank

God every day for them because I know He sent them so that I would not get lost in the process.

I even began to do new things I would never do, like connecting with nature. I take walks on the beach, hike, swim in lakes, stand on mountains to view the horizon, etc. I never knew how peaceful and rewarding it was until I tried it. I think I find a piece of me every time I take a chance in life. Give it a try because you never know what you will find along the way. There are many groups within your community that you can join so you do not feel alone if you do not like to do things alone. You will be surprised that there is something for everyone.

Now that I am healed, I can properly pour my experiences into my patients, friends, family, and whoever else God sends my way. Remember, forgiveness is the first true step towards healing. When we are healed, we can see with the correct perspective and respond with love and kindness in all types of situations. I have found purpose in helping others to start their healing journey and I love every minute of it. If you had told me years ago, that I would be living fulfilled and happy in my God-given purpose, I would not have believed it because of all the pain I endured. God truly does work everything out for our good if you allow Him. Trust God with all of you and every experience. He has the power to help you change, grow, and get back on track.

Chapter 6

The Journey to Recovery

In this section, you will have a chance to write down any questions, concerns, and thoughts. Writing is an important part of healing because this type of therapy enables you to release things in private until you can talk it over with someone. You have the chance to tell your truth without feeling fear or judgment. After you have released it on paper, it will give your mind more freedom to process what happened to you. Then I would suggest you pray about the situation and ask God to heal you. God can perform a miraculous healing for you, or He may give you steps to follow. Keep in mind everyone's healing process is different and every process has its own turnaround time. The most important part is that you start the process and do not stop until it is finished. Whatever steps God gives you, just obey even if it seems crazy. He does want the best for His people.

I just want to say that I am proud of you for getting this far in your process. Taking the first step is the hardest, but once you accomplish that it only gets easier with every step thereafter. I have been there and can only give you something I had to live through. I made it and I have hope and faith that you will too. You can do this! Remember, fear only comes to stop and block you, but do it afraid anyway.

Below is a list of healing strategies I recommend:

1. Writing/ Journaling
2. Talk Therapy

3. Psychotherapy, DBT

4. Trauma-Based Therapy

5. Cryotherapy; if safe EMDR

6. Hypnotherapy

7. Acupuncture

8. Healing Childhood Trauma

9. Exercising

10. Meditation on God's Word

11. Prayer

12. Build a Healthy Community

13. Self-Care, including eating healthy

14. Self-Love

Look over the list of healing strategies and circle the recommendations you are willing to try, then do your research. Are you willing to factor them into your schedule today? If so, how would you apply them to your life? Write a detailed plan to help you stay dedicated and focused.

_____

_____

_____

_____

_____

_____

_____

_____

_____

_____

_____

_____

_____

_____

_____

_____

_____

_____

_____

Scriptures I like to meditate on as I am stretching, praying, and exercising:

"For I know the plans I have for you," declares the LORD, "plans to prosper you and not to harm you, plans to give you hope and a future."
Jeremiah 29:11 NIV

"And we know that in all things God works for the good of those who love him, who have been called according to his purpose."
Romans 8:28 NIV

"No weapon forged against you will prevail, and you will refute every tongue that accuses you. This is the heritage of the servants of the LORD, and this is their vindication from me," declares the LORD."
Isaiah 54:17 NIV

"And my God will meet all your needs according to the riches of his glory in Christ Jesus." Philippines 4:19 NIV

Recovery

Starting over can be hard, but it is not impossible. We all go through different journeys in different chapters of our lives. Do not rush the process but embrace every moment of it. There is always a lesson to learn. Every model is generally the same. There is trauma or abuse on one end and healing on the other, but no one really talks about what happens in between. In the middle, a death of some sort takes place, but it is a unique death which varies one person to the next. You will then notice the five stages of grief according to the Kübler-Ross model, which are denial, anger, bargaining, depression, and acceptance. I found myself in each of these stages fighting for my life in the middle. Before I became healed, many things in my life had to die like trauma bounds, generational curses, toxic thinking, codependency, low self-esteem, pride, bitterness, resentment, abandonment, neglect, rejection, childhood trauma, negative speech, etc. I had to embrace the road to recovery. I have children who look up to me and depend on me. Most importantly I needed healing and wholeness for myself. Below are eleven principles to recover from a narcissistic or toxic relationship:

11 Principles to Recover from a Narcissistic Toxic Relationship

1. Live in reality instead of just settling to exist in someone else's world. Some things are out of your control. Learn to be okay with that.
2. Don't wait for opportunities to come your way. Instead, go after what you want.
3. Prioritize your health.
4. Take time to self-reflect and do not miss the moments to stop and smell the roses.
5. Change your perspective and language because you will attract what you speak. Therefore, learn to only speak positive even in the midst of a storm.
6. Get out into nature and explore new things and hobbies.
7. Do not abandon your needs, wants, or likes. Learn to put yourself first and love yourself.
8. Build confidence and financial independence.
9. Do not wait for an apology because it may never happen.
10. Detach from the stories and self-limiting beliefs.
11. Forgive them and yourself and release the shame, guilt, and hurt.

Create a list that includes things you like to do along with new things you would like to try. Don't be shy! Step out on faith and mark it down on your calendar. Do not second guess it, just do it! Go with the flow. If you do not like the new thing you tried, it's ok. You created a memory to look back and say you had the courage to try something new.

_____

_____

_____

_____

_____

_____

_____

_____

_____

_____

Are You New to Relationships?

Watch out for red flags or caution signs while getting to know someone. They can serve as insight into a person's character. It is easy to get comfortable with the "good" in others, so we tend to ignore the flaws. Do not go into a situation thinking you can change someone! The flaws are there for you to see and judge if you can tolerate them in your life or not. People only change when they are ready and there is nothing you can say or do to change that. Do not get caught up in trying to take control of someone else's life. The only one you can control is YOU. The only one you can fix is YOU.

The danger in overlooking red flags or seeing them and trying to change someone is you become drained, taken advantage of, and abused. Your expectations will never be met! You then find yourself emotionally attached and invested in someone who isn't into you, isn't worthy of you or your time, or just isn't the right fit for you. It is safe to assume that someone just getting to know you is on their best behavior. Therefore, if you see the red flags within the first few dates or conversations, their behavior is highly likely to get worse in the future. Be observant and take your time. God will send the "RIGHT" one your way.

According to relationship experts, these are red flags you should look out for when dating someone new:

Love bombing
Moving too quickly
Not introducing you to their friends or family
Gaslighting
Inconsistent behavior
Ignore or have a problem with your boundaries
You don't like their friends
You recognize their stories do not add up or you spot a lie

They guilt trip or manipulate you into doing things outside of your boundaries

They go silent for long periods between conversations

They make harsh jokes that hurt your feelings

Angry outburst about small things

They constantly bring up their ex

Have a parent who is controlling or disrespectful

They always look for their friend's approval

They dwell on traumatic things in their past

Think and speak negative often

Jealousy

Controlling

Gets physical in a negative manner

Trauma Bonding

Take a moment to look over these red flags and note if you ever experienced any of them. Then note how long you tolerated the red flags before the relationship was over and why?

_____

_____

_____

_____

_____

_____

_____

_____

_____

_____

_____

_____

_____

Now, write down an action plan. Would you change anything during your course of dating, courtship, or "getting to know you" phase? If so, what would it be?

_____

_____

_____

_____

_____

_____

_____

_____

_____

Keep in mind, healthy boundaries are the way to go. Don't try to make them up as you go because it will be easy to get manipulated by someone and hard to stay consistent with your boundaries. If you are not consistent with them, why would the person you are dating respect them? They will not take you seriously if they see your boundaries are optional.

Think about what makes you happy and brings you peace. Those will be the boundaries you want to enforce with everyone you meet. Write down your boundaries below and practice them. The more you practice, the more natural it will become, and you will grow in confidence.

_____

_____

_____

_____

_____

_____

I would like to close this book out with "The Serenity Prayer" because it brings life into a better and clearer perspective as I meditate on these words. Perhaps it will do the same for you.

The Serenity Prayer

God grant me the serenity

to accept the things I cannot change;

courage to change the things I can;

and wisdom to know the difference.

Living one day at a time;

Enjoying one moment at a time;

Accepting hardships as the pathway to peace;

Taking, as He did, this sinful world

as it is, not as I would have it;

Trusting that He will make all things right

if I surrender to His Will;

That I may be reasonably happy in this life

and supremely happy with Him

Forever in the next.

Amen.

Did this prayer change your perspective or outlook on life, relationships, family, dreams, goals, etc.? If so, how? If not, why? Write down your response.

_____

_____

_____

_____

_____

_____

_____

_____

_____

_____

_____

_____

_____

When life spins out of control, take a moment to think about the words to this prayer. Hopefully, it will help you to navigate through your situation with wisdom. I pray this prayer helps you to accept the things you can not change in life and build the courage to change the things you can!

www.ingramcontent.com/pod-product-compliance
Lightning Source LLC
Chambersburg PA
CBHW071017120626
46546CB00003B/1123